10 STUPID THINGS married women say & do

Moss Mashamaite

redOystor

London | Johannesburg | New York

Copyright © 2018 Moss Mashamaite

First Published by ChatWorld Publishing 2006
Second Publication by RedOystor Books 2018
    an Imprint of RedOystor Media (Pty) Ltd
    with permission from Moss & Moss Publishing

All rights reserved. No part of this publication may be reproduced, stored in a retrieval system, or transmitted in any form or by any means, electronic, mechanical, photocopying, recording, or otherwise, be lent, re-sold, hired-out, or otherwise circulated without express written consent of the author.

Published by RedOystor Books
an imprint of RedOystor Media (Pty) Ltd

visit www.redoystor.com for more information
Or contact us at **www.redoystor.com/contact-us**

www.redoystor.com/TenStupidThingsWoman
www.facebook.com/TenStupidThing

Cover Design & Layout by **RedOystor Media (Pty) Ltd**

Printed by **novus print**, a Novus Holdings company

Available on Kindle and other retail outlets

ISBN: 978-0-9947217-8-5 (Print)
      978-0-9947217-9-2 (eBook)

It's Official! There Is No Cure For Stupidity

Contents

Acknowledgments	iii
Dedication	v
Warning	vii
Wanted! A cure for Stupidity	1
One: Becoming a Mamma	23
Two: I Have a Headache	47
Three: Wena le Sokhanyana ye ya gago	65

Four: Your Mamma   **79**

Five: Trying To Look Good To Your Kids At
The Expense Of Their Father   **95**

Six: Where are you at?   **107**

Seven: BEIJING   **119**

Eight: Threatening Your Man With Divorce
                                                          143

Nine: Blar, Blar, Blar... Write your own **159**

Ten: TRYING TO CHANGE YOUR MAN   **163**

About: The Author   **179**
Other Stupid Books   **185**

Acknowledgments

A Woman's book written by a man needs a woman editor for sure. I think I picked the best of the crop. Intelligent, keen-spirited, witty and highly opinionated.

I am grateful for all the fights we've had over the content and diction and I would like to thank Faith Mbili, for a splendid job.

I would also like to acknowledge the following people for their assistance, contributions and encouragement in writing and publishing yet another one of my 'stupid' books - Sam Ramenu, Busisiwe B. Mahlangu, Tshegwane Mohapi, Success Moagi, Elias Letshoene, Kelebogile Mashokwe, Jacob T. Mashamaite, Sarah Jeanelize De Bruin, Rev. Phillip G. Hlungwani, Mokgadi Mathonzi, Papi Mathonzi and Olive Daba. You have contributed in making my thoughts on this subject level with reality.

How could I ever write a book with such wide nuances and broad intimations all by myself? I've had to put my theories in the crucible of other people's experiences and observations.

To write a book with merit on married people one must talk to unmarried women, unmarried men, married women, married men, divorced women, divorced men, widows, widowers, bachelors, spinsters, married and single children.

DEDICATION

To my aunt Olive R. Daba - my mother's little sister. Olive was married to her husband Boy Daba for twenty five years. For twenty five years she woke up everyday to give her husband 'coffee in bed'. Where she learnt that from, I wouldn't know, because where she grew up coffee was a luxury that was enjoyed on Christmas and New Year's Day only.

The one thing I know is, her husband didn't ask or insist on it, she just did it. I told a young bride this story and the first thing she said was, 'It's a cute little story, as long as I am not expected to do that.'

First stupid thing a young wife said and did. She went totally defensive and berserk. She was simply saying, 'Beijing, expect nothing!' Women hate men who expect things, I know that.

My uncle wasn't expecting, my aunt was just serving. The other side of the story that she told me was that the returns she had for that unusual act of romance and devotion were amazing.

Warning

This book is rated PG. Parental guidance is advised.

Before you read each chapter call your parents and tell them what you are about to read. Ask them to guide you. When they have thoroughly guided you, read.

After you have read call your parents again. This time irate. Ask them why they never told you all these things before. After you finish reading this book, call your college or university principal and ask for a discount on your education.

Ask him/her why they did not include a course on marriage and being a married woman when this was such an important eventuality in your life. If he/she refuses with a discount call me. Since at this time your airtime would be depleted, send me a 'please call me' - I might just return your call.

I think it's the duty of the comedian to find out where the line is drawn and cross it deliberately
 – George Carlin

Wanted!

A Cure for Stupidity

'We do not have to visit a madhouse to find disordered minds. Our planet is the mental institution of the universe' - not my words, but the person who said them needs to get into my WhatsApp group.

I surfed the Internet, scoured through the Encyclopedia Britannica, even ransacked the dusty pages of the Bible. I plunged into the Al Quran and fumbled through the Bhagavad-Gita. I peered into the Wisdom of Solomon and Confucius and I was left solemn and confused. I called friends and relatives; acquaintances and enemies. I consulted witchdoctors, pharmacists, and alchemists, even politicians, and robbers. I inquired of prophets and idiots, even certified lunatics.

All in search of What? A Cure! A cure for Stupidity.

I got no joy out of my quest. I called a committee and summoned a tribunal, I invited brilliant minds into a commission of inquiry and nobody pitched. That's when I decided - it's official! There is no cure for stupidity!

What qualifies me to write a book for women

The day that I announced on the radio that I was going to write this stupid book, I received a couple of heated emails and calls from my married women friends. They were unanimous in their opinion about my lack of qualification to write on such an important top.

Their notion, if I might add is, if I felt inclined to contribute in this field of human endeavour, I should rather write a book addressed to men — their men.

I took some time to ponder over the suggestion. After much thought I decided they were right, the man side of this book was much more urgent. However, agreeing with them does not necessarily mean I should comply. Since I did take the route they had suggested I must explain, lest someone complains to the broadcasting commission of black twitter.

Women might want to know why I wrote about them and not about their men. The reasons are as follows:

I was raised in a family that had both parents.

Though I have some experience raising a woman – with my daughter, I know that women are doing it every day in greater numbers with greater success. While at it, many of these women work their pretty butts off to make their marriages successful.

Their husbands sit aside reading a newspaper while waiting for the next game of sports to go with a hot home-cooked meal. This indicates that women are mostly better, and myself, involved parents than men are. I have been a single father for a couple years now and nobody in the world appreciates mothers and what they go through more than I do.

I doff my hat to all mothers. I thought I was a great and dedicated father until I was left alone when my dear wife passed on. Only then did I realize that it was great motherhood that made my part-time fatherhood look like the real thing. I also know that many a marriage has survived the stupidity of men, but if women become stupid, entire families will collapse – guaranteed!

Whether we want to admit to it or not, we live in a matriarchal society. Men might be the heads but women are the rest of the body. So, just in case you are wondering, I didn't write this book because I have 'beef' with women. I wrote it because I wanted to strengthen the strongest link of every marriage before I deal with the weakest link.

I may be playing to the stereotypical generalization of men, but for the purposes of this book, allow me to insult your intelligence.

I know there are some brilliant fathers and husbands out there. Nevertheless, this is half a book, the other half will be written in consultation with some of the greatest women I know.

As for this stupid book, I think I am fully qualified to write it. I have been married twice, I failed the first time. All me. My fault entirely. I was the head of the family and as many reasons as I could advance to you, I am the one who failed.

Second marriage - a great success. It was the most beautiful interpersonal experience I've ever had. The kind of relationship you cannot afford to be stupid about. If I fail I learn. Once again credit should not all be given to me, I was married to my soul mate, and what a soul; and what a mate!

I have since married again to a beautiful soul. Nothing compares when love connects with the soul.

You know, they say every great person should have at least three lifetimes. You can ask Tata Madiba about that when you cross the great beyond - I'm sure he has stories for days. But my third time has been a charm. In my third and hopefully final marriage I have found a soul. Someone I can connect with on so many levels. With these experiences, I can safely say I have the certificate to pen this thesis of stupidity for married women.

I write because I can

I am not writing this book because of the sudden itch of the pen.

I have gazed into the depths of this relationship called marriage and I've seen women bleed and men cry and though my style is light, even humorous, I know that my subject is not a laughing matter.

I was raised within a marriage so I might even be doing this for your kids. Sometimes even if you don't have much in life, there's one thing you need to know; a happy marriage can do your children a great deal of good.

Just one happy couple can create balance in the lives of kids and even turn them into great people.

When I was a boy Pastor I hated doing counselling, especially for married people. I simply thought I wasn't equipped or yet qualified to give guidance on a matter I had little or no experience with.

What was I going to tell them if I hadn't experienced it?

Besides, I was almost a virgin and sex is one of the bigger problems in marriage, and they still brought to the sessions such issues as sexual dysfunctions or deprivations. I am sure by now you are asking yourself, 'what do you mean — almost a virgin'

'You are either one or not.'

I am sorry but that is my story, and I am sticking to it—I was almost a virgin. I am still not fond of relationship or marital counselling.

Having written this book, you would think I relish the opportunity to engage with to you and your husband about the challenges of your relationship – that's not me.

That said, I have to admit I know several therapists who would like that. I converse with a lot of them. Occasionally I sit in some of their group sessions.

Trust me! With such connections I have come to appreciate the delicate intricacies of relationships.

Qualified by Experience

The funny thing is, in all my years as an unmarried Pastor, only one man ever came to me with a 'real' marital problem he needed me to help resolve. As predictable a species as men are — I soon came to realise it was about a sexual dysfunction. I may be considered a Doctor now with my doctorate and all, but back then even such accolades were not suited for the qualifications – his problem needed a medical doctor not a spiritual theologian.

The idea that he believed I was well suited to solve his problem gave me great hope, but that he brought it to me when I was only a single young man, '*almost a virgin*', means that he needed a miracle – a BIG miracle.

I remember he was the religious type and had such conservative theories about sex. I shudder just thinking about it. As I was expounding my book knowledge on the act of love, he was shocked by most of the things I said. I was also shocked about how much I knew about something I *knew* very little about or had limited real life experience with.

Missionaries on a sex mission

As it so happened, he thought the only position permissible in his bedroom relations was that one where the woman poses like a Nando's full chicken – obviously not cut in 8 pieces – favoured in lemon and herb, definitely not hot - the famous *missionary position*.

Speaking of the 'missionary' position, I was so fascinated with the name that decided to do some research on it.

I brought this research knowledge to one of our counselling sessions. I explained to him that the missionary position was the most popular love making position of the ancient Greek and Roman cultures, a nine out of ten favourite.

These two cultures became the influences of European culture which carried the gospel of Christ into the world. Now when the missionaries came to Africa, the Americas, the East and other countries, they found out that the natives made love in ways they regarded as bizarre, even traumatizing to their mental sexual template.

Through religious indoctrination, we were force to believe our ways in coitus was unholy. They then gave us a love making template of the ancient Greek which they called the *'missionary position'* to save us from dirty sex and certain damnation.

Talking about dirty sex, I believe it was Woody Allen who asked and answered himself "Is sex dirty?" His response was "Only if it's done right." I opened the scriptures in the book of Genesis and I said to him, 'Firstly, the Bible just commands us to be fruitful and multiply without a 'How-to Manual' attached to this command.

Forget the crusade

"Isn't it curious though that the first commandment that God ever gave to mankind was to copulate until the entire earth is fully populated? Don't you think that God is mighty glad with the Chinese?" His eyes almost popped out of their sockets when I shared this observation.

I continued, "The good book also says, 'Adam knew his wife…'

I told him that "to know one's wife" is a mouthful, one's got to be very thorough to achieve that. You've got to explore territories and frontiers of her body and her sexuality that the writers of sex manuals do not even know exist.

"To know", you might have to research, which includes asking the right questions - to explore and discover, which might also mean touching the right places, all places; and loving it.

I spoke like one possessed by the goddess of sex. When I was through with him he went home to open new chapters in the vast book of sexuality that was his wife. He came back to me a happy face, and asked me, 'How did you know all that?'

Of course I did not answer, I could indict myself. If I had mentioned experience he would have doubted my devotion to God, being a religious type. If I had cited the library, he would not trust my authority and he could lose the lesson. So I just smiled at him and said, 'I am glad I could help.' The magician does not reveal his tricks. Other than this man, it's only been women who have availed themselves for a bettering of their lives and relationships. That is why I am writing the women book first.

Another reason I wrote the women book first is because I know women. If I wrote the man book first, women would buy the book for their men with ulterior motives. And knowing men and their egos, I doubt they would read it – unless I changed the title to 'How to be a god in the Bedroom'.

We all know that would be stupid and I have no intentions of being stupid about this stupid book. Besides, it would be like preparing counselling sessions that have been initiated by a woman.

A *'typical'* man – and I use the word typical very loosely here – would attend the session but shut off as soon as he gets there. Pray God the therapist is not a woman from Beijing, or a cleaned up male cutie who sounds like his parents paid a fortune for his education. Then the man doesn't just shut off, he expires.

Trading places

After reading any of my 'Ten Stupid Things' titles you might be tempted to think, 'What is this Jack of all trades now going to say this time around?' Before you even get there, let me inform you that my elder brother's name is Jack, not me; and besides none of the things I write about are trades. So, Jack of all trades, Me? No way.

Next you will ask yourself, but he is a man. Yes, I am a *dude* and this dude thinks he is a better expert writing this book than he would be writing its opposite.

I am duly qualified...

My friend Rev. Phillip Hlungwani preached a powerful sermon many years ago at a wedding, entitled: "If I was a Married Woman." It was probably the best sermon I had ever heard preached in my life on the subject of women and marriage.

So I am saying, I am better at this because of the view from where I stand. A football coach might not be the best player and actually might have never played the beautiful game professionally, but he has got the better view of the game.

His mind is not cluttered with detail. He sees the bigger picture and the unfolding of the game. Therefore, he is best suited to coach the players and tell them what they can do better if they are to win the game.

I have known married women in my life. I was married *thrice* – if there is such a word; but because my spell checker didn't underline it in red, I'll take it I am good to continue.

I was raised by a married woman, and both my sisters and first cousins are all married women, almost all. I work with married women, and I used to be a Pastor for about ten years and in my church like in most other churches, there were more married women than there were men and I interacted with them a lot.

Women, I prayed with and for them, gave them tissues for their issues as they wiped their salty waters. So get off my case.

Just take it from me, I am qualified to write this book. Not because I have a little bit of English to play around with, but because I should know what I am talking about.

...Because I write stupid books.

After reading "Ten Stupid Things Young People Say and Do," a very excited friend of mine said to me that I should write a lot of 'Stupid books.' He suggested I also write Ten Stupid Things Couples Say and Do. I said, 'No, I can't.' He asked why. I said, 'Men are from Mars and women are from Venus.' Men and women are so different you can't quite write a marriage book for them together.

We use different toilets, different soaps, different lotions and on this one, we are going to have to use different books.

Looking at life and the institution of marriage from my rear view mirror, I must say I have seen and heard a lot of stupid things.

'From where?' You ask.

From South Africa and everywhere. Remember that I am a man, a husband, a son, an employer, a friend, a neighbour, many things to many people, like I have already mentioned. Over and above that, I have been around the block a couple of times. I have also used up my return ticket from hell; been there and back – got the t-shirt; but that came from heaven.

So I have heard lots and lots; and lots of stupid things.

Some of the stupid things I have heard in South Africa are the names of informal settlements, also known as squatter camps.

The funny thing about the names is that they have social tones to them, and I am not being derogatory, God forbid!

Names like '*Hlala Mpja*' (Divorce The Dog); implying that most people who live there are women who've had to divorce a legal-wise unworthy man or dog.

Names like '*Serope Mperekele*' (which means 'Thigh, work for me'). Meaning, the inhabitants of the *squatter camp* are mostly single women who live off other women's men. Names like '*Dunusa*' (Bend Over) - I know you know what that means.

I wrote a piece in a novel about my favourite squatter camp '*Skuurlik*' and how it came to be. Of all the stupid things you can do for yourself, this you have to read.

Skuurlik is my favourite squatter camp because it's not judgmental of the people who live there like *Hlala Mpja*! The name simply reflects the pace of its development as a residential area.

Somebody told me the other day when I was struggling to complete a project that, 'Rome was not built in a day.'

I said but Skuurlik was. The reason why 'Rome was not built in a day' is only because they did not have a South African telephone directory then.

The Story Skuurlik

Skuurlik is an Afrikaans word meaning, *suddenly!!!* (With three exclamation marks - that sudden). Although black people, especially the less fortunate lot pretend to hate Afrikaans, their choice of words and names always make one wonder. How the name Skuurlik came into being is rather amusing. Legend has it that some guy, a prospective resident went home to the Northern Cape on a Friday morning. He came back the Sunday and found a whole *brand new* village standing solidly on the shoulders of the formal Mamelodi township.

The new villagers walked about in a relaxed manner of such as were born and bred above the self-same soil. Their neighbours, the formally settled *Mamelodians* nevertheless eyed them narrowly as if there was some stench to them, but they couldn't care less.

Amongst them, entertainers, were already running generators and playing loud music of all genres. Drunks, intoxicated by all sorts of inebriating liquids, including anything from Whiskey to home brewed beer, not excluding *Listerine* mouthwash which boasts about thirty percent alcohol content - all staggering around in a rural elderly manner.

Standing at the street corners were already cleaned up, sunlight washed boys dressed in expensive branded clothes, more expensive than the houses they were standing next to, propositioning beautiful well-groomed and nicely dressed young maidens, promising anything from heaven to nirvana.

The maidens being great of faith, believing every promise as if it were from the mouths of the gods.

The very same Sunday, second day of residence in Skuurlik, there were already several church services in session. There was one in particular where the parson preached with such energy he tore the cotton shelter apart, such that his sermon deviated as he began to preach about the torn cloth.

A sermon that had neither God nor sense in it, yet was very pleasing to the ears of the sparse congregation, especially the pair of ears attached to the head that pronounced the wordy oration, if generosity of diction could stretch its kindly arms and embrace the wordy soliloquy as such.

On this Sunday of unworthy wordy sermons, this *Northern Caper* - himself a frolicker - joined the entertainers, the entertained and the drunks, and became one with them and spoke in his drunken Northern Cape ways saying to the nearest pair of ears, "*Hey my broertjie, die plek neh, het net Skuurlik opgespring.*" His fellow drunk said from the other side. "*Hey, mona ke Skuurlik le a utlwa, jy het ham my broer.*"

Even as this Northern Cape gentleman was walking home to a back-room in Mamelodi, planning how to come and join the new residents - he staggered carefully lest he be spotted as one thoroughly taken by the grip of happy waters, and therefore be taken advantage of.

He had lost several cell phones to polite muggers when he was drunk and staggering. They would politely ask for his cell phone, but he knew that behind the polite request lay an unequaled ruthlessness.

As he walked, there was this gentleman standing at the corner of a meandering street looking to and fro like he was afraid of something. He was also chewing gum ferociously, like the gum was serving a life sentence.

He wondered in how a man could already have committed an act that caused guilt and fear in such a '*Skuurlike nuweplekkie*'

His thoughts drifted back to his ambition of finding a piece of real estate in this great new place.

He had a cousin who knew somebody who knew somebody who could hook him up with somebody who could hook him up with a spot. A piece of undeclared real estate that could be sold by somebody who didn't own it.

So one by one, the happy people left for their respective homes in and out of Skuurlik.

When the drunken party had dispersed to share the joys of the nameless place where they had watered their throats with joy, they all spread the '*Skuurlik*' name like bees would pollen in the summer.

When Monday came along so blue, the place was christened *Skuurlik* and everybody already knew that, as though it had been announced on a popular radio talk-show like Taba-Kgolo of Thobela FM

Don't mind the stupidity

Squatter camps have the most stupid names and yet the most honest. Take '*Hlala Mpja*' as a case in point, in there live women who used to be happily married to some legal-wise men until they did several stupid things; and others who, although not sophisticated enough to compete with you in anything, including English and hygiene. They are sleeping with your husband and making him wonder what he is doing in an unhappy mansion in the suburbs when the shack seems so pleasant an environment.

I don t mean you should go and buy unleaded petrol and burn up shacks, I am just telling the truth as I know it. I am also not saying what I have said is true of all women who live there, not even half of it, but and a big BUT - you sure do get my drift, don't you?

Skuurlik is a metaphor for quickly arranged marriages and haphazardly run families with women who are pushing the economic trolleys with little care for the other facets of married life. *Skuurlik* represents reckless abandonment and the stupidity of building a home on undeclared land.

There is a house and then there is a home. Most married women who will read this book - on the house side of things - do really good. They live in plush surroundings with luxurious furnishings, but on the home side of things, they might as well live in *Skuurlik*.

It's a squatter camp and you know it. Your man is squatting, you are squatting and so are your children. You live in *Skuurlik* next door to *Hlala Mpja*.

Now allow me to reduce our great parable to a metaphor. I am going to use the name *Skuurlik* throughout this book and every time I do, you must understand the *Skuurlik* image and go with the flow.

Skuurlik from now on ceases to be an Afrikaans word. *Skuurlik* becomes our metaphor and an English word. As a poet I do not only have poetic license, I can create English words even without the permission of the Queen of England, it's a perk, comes with the job.

The Downside Doozy

I have been to the divorce court once, it is the saddest place on planet earth, where the phrase 'I do' is replaced with, 'What the hell did I do?'

I am sure you think the saddest place on planet earth must be the graveyard. I have been to the graveyard and I've been to the divorce court. From experience I will tell you this free-of-charge with a discount - the graveyard was sad and very painful. I had lost my soul mate, but two years later I had healed. She had gone to another life, a better life, the way of all the earth. My love for her and her love for me will remain forever, and one day we will meet and all the pain with its residues will go away.

There is healing inherent in the system especially if you were in love, adored and served, and were devoted to each other. There is closure with the graveyard and even a future in the after-life.

The divorce court on the other hand is a totally different situation. In there are couples who mostly do not hate each other but simply can't live together. Most people are there not because love died, but because love is immortal. They are there because *stupid things* came in the way of *important things* and each one of the parties involved decided to go and pursue happiness elsewhere, and often alone.

This book is also for Married woman with Stupid ideas

This is a woman's book and I will therefore be very direct to women.

Fact: women lose their men mostly for stupid reasons. Most women realise a couple of years later when they get to meet other men that they actually had a good deal, a better deal.

It goes something like this: She loves the dude, he's cool and he makes her laugh. She goes out with him, she gives him all the things that make men happy – including freedom.

He can go out as he pleases and see his friends and breath the Friday evening oxygen, which by the way is the best oxygen any man has ever breathed.

He likes the way she is free-spirited and liberating to his soul. He marries her in an elaborate wedding-of-the-year affair or at Home Affairs – whichever tickles his pockets. He might also choose to make vows before a preacher or gets the families together for the *lobola* and traditional ceremony. Doesn't matter how he does it, what matters is that he choose you. Bottom line she marries him.

Then suddenly she thinks, "holy sh#t - some woman might want to grab him." He is a rare species. Let me tie him up in my house. Let me make sure that his trips are between work and home. Let me limit his delegated responsibilities to church and funeral - who ever's funeral it might be.

Make sure he attends the funeral of anybody who dies within a radius of three hundred kilometers, and be with him in a nasty black outfit making sure every other woman knows that this one is married. Make sure I put tabs on him like the FBI on some middle-eastern terrorist studying in some American community college.

I must know where his potentially philanderous arse is - always. I am going to become a prison warder and this *man* will become my prisoner - Prisoner No: 32146 - till death do us part.

BUT there are two things this kind of woman forgets:

>> Prisoners do escape and,

>> There are other things that could do people part other than death - I've been to the divorce court once, and I've seen people part still breathing. So till death do us part is not the final word.

I've lived in America and in some cities like Los Angeles they actually rent out wedding rings. They have seen enough people parting - before death does them apart - and some smart guy decided, 'Hey, we could rent these things out and that would mean more money for us.

I mean marriage is not permanent anymore.

We would still own the rings while the temporary arrangements pay us for their use. Actually in my opinion, a prison break should not be regarded as a crime. It's as natural as the need for a bird to fly.

Nobody wants to live in confinement.

If you have ever been to jail even for a visit, you will know that there is only one desire in the heart of any prisoner - to get out. Any woman who wants to jail her man or cut his legs, must just know one thing for sure, your prisoner is thinking about one thing, and one thing only — how to break out and break free.

His only mission is prison break.

The thing about imprisonment is that it makes people very resourceful. How do you think people in jail get drugs, guns, whiskey - single malt! They have by reason of imprisonment become the most resourceful beings on earth.

If one day a pretty, drop dead gorgeous girl emerges out of your pantry, you must know that you have created a cheating genius out of your man by incarcerating him.

Good Marriage- it is Possible

So what are you going to do? When I was still a Pastor I used to advise women to pray for their men. Right now I think I will leave that advice for your pastor.

I don't mean there is anything wrong with praying for your man – now turned Prisoner No: 32146. But I must say, your prayer should never become a substitute for things you can do by yourself.

Prayer is simply asking God to do the impossible for you. I am sure He would be willing to do the *'impossible'* as long as you are willing to do the *possible*.

This book is not about to help you perform the impossible. It will persuade you to do what is possible, and that is sufficient to turn any marriage around.

Now let's leave church alone.

Let's have a heart to heart talk.

I want you to feel my heart as you go through the pages of this book. You will be delighted, even annoyed by my brutal honesty. I do not like when people read any of my books without emotion. If you are to thoroughly enjoy this book, you must please me by connecting emotionally to the subject at hand.

I must make you laugh, but I also must make you angry, I simply cannot leave you without emotion.

That is just the way I communicate.

When you get to the end of this book you will be glad you bought it but more so because read it till the end. You may end up feeling like you hate me or even love me; or love to hate me.

If by then, you have decided to love me, drop me an email at DrMoss@mossandmoss.co.za.

Should you decide you hate me or love to hate me, that is still acceptable. It is the result of many honest relationships.

Before the WARNING

Remember life is all about relationships. If you are unhappy in a relationship you are an unhappy person. There are no unhappily married happy people. Period. That's why I tell readers in my "Ten Stupid Things Single People Say and Do," that the decision to get married is perhaps one of the three most important decisions of your life.

When you do that, you are voting on your happiness or your unhappiness, nothing more, nothing less. So when you are married you are going to have to push the happiness deal.

I hope reading this book will add to your account of marital bliss, which is by the way the most important account, because most, if not everything in your life might just depend on that.

This book is about ten things that put the greatest strain on marriages. In all the chapters of this book I will be addressing those things. Every stupid thing represents something serious enough to reduce your level of enjoyment for each other. In some chapters I lump several stupid things up.

You will also realize that I did not single out the usual culprits that are often brought up in marital counselling sessions, namely - communication and finance. It's because I sought a fresh approach and this is not a marriage counselling book or a couple's book. It's your book and I want it to uniquely address and help you.

I have tried to talk about things most people will miss out which are stupid yet very critical to know. I have a chapter on sex, on the umbilical crowd, mostly known as the in-laws. I have addressed the usual abandonment of the self as soon as women get married, encouraging self-improvement in all regards, physical, mental, financial and spiritual.

I have seriously attacked the 50/50 approach to marriage that was given birth to in 1995 - Beijing. I have also looked at the total invasion of personal space that is brought about in marriage - with the invention the cellphone and other technologies.

I've addressed problems of insecurity and the spirit of competition between lovers and many other things that you'd have to dig out with your eyes as you go through the journey of this book.

Marriage can be the saddest relationship of them all, yet it can also be the happiest. Most people live in the middle of these two extreme emotions with an occasional high and an occasional low.

The wisdom shared in this book can steer your marriage, through the educating of even half the marital person which is yourself, to more highs and to above average.

I take marriage very seriously; I wish all people did. When you get into marriage get in and use every tool, every good and useful advice you can get to make your love relationship a nursery and an example for your children, so they come out of it into the world as giants.

I love Mark Twain's encouragement towards serious living. He says, "I respect the man who knows distinctly what he wishes. The greater part of all mischief in the world arises from the fact men do not sufficiently understand their own aims. They have undertaken to build a tower, and yet spend no more labour on the foundation than would be necessary to erect a hut."

WARNING

This book is for only those women who were chosen by their men to become their wives.

If you manipulated your man into marrying you, this book is not going to help you at all because the way you got your man is basically the same way you are going to have to keep him.

If you got him through manipulation you are going to have to manipulate your way into marital bliss if that is even possible.

If you bewitched him into matrimony you are going to have to continue to use your witchcraft throughout. And with modern witchcraft let us hope for your sake, that you monthly subscription to the 'Keep your man plan' is up to date and paid up.

If he was married and you snatched him from another woman through divorce you might have to live your entire life haunted by the other woman.

This is the karma of every married woman.

But wait! There's more.

I have a magical wand that can reverse even the harshest laws of karma. It's called grace and it dictates as follows - 'What happened yesterday does not necessarily have to determine your tomorrows.'

It is the concept that was introduced to this world by the Apostle Paul.

By the grace of our Lord, all is forgiven and the future belongs to those who will decide to create it. No matter what ghost haunts your nights and what ogres terrorize your day - this book can turn your life around.

There is a cure for stupidity.

People and marriages can be delivered from yesterday's curses.

There is always hope for a person who can pick up a book and read. Not only read, but also apply themselves to the new found knowledge of this book.

I wrote a little poem for you and I hope you enjoy it, it's entitled 'Let us love as love does.'

An Ode to Love

Let us love with no mention of marriage so grave
Let us love for the sake of love itself
Let us love with the gay abandon of doves
Let us love keenly as love only can
Let us love like there is no tomorrow
Then when tomorrow comes
And love has consummated itself
Let us bury our affections in an institution
The institution of marriage so fair and final

Then let us love till grey death do us part
And hope that nothing will come 'tween us
And do death's dirty job
Then let us love to the enjoyment of our true selves
Let us love till kingdom come
Let us love until our love a kingdom builds
And make of us a king and a queen
And our home a castle and

Our offspring, princes and princesses
Let us love and not look back
Let us love and teach each other
To look at each other and spite distractions
Those optical delusions that betray the eye
Let us love as if love out of fashion went
Let us love till love is blind and make sure
That there is no cure for the blindness so dark
Let us love till there's no place for anything else
Till we enjoy to live in an institution's long as its name is love
Let us love because we are creatures of love

Created by love and raised by love
To love without sense or reason
Let us love and sing the anthem of life
Let us love to the exhaustion of love's fountains deep
And discover for ourselves their bottomlessness

Let us love and sing the song that awakens imaginations
Let us write a story that will make a fairy tale
A love that will make fairy tales come true
Let us love like there is indeed no tomorrow

"Negligence is the rust of the soul, that corrodes through all her best resolves"
- *Owen Feltham*

Remember life is all about relationships. If you are unhappy in a relationship you are an unhappy person. There are no unhappily married happy people. Period.

One

BECOMING A MAMMA

Most women think as soon as they have kids they can change their state of being like tadpoles change into frogs, and larva into butterflies.

They think they can change from girlfriend and wife to become Johnny's mother.

I admit that there is nothing wrong with being *uMama-ka-Johnny*. That in itself is a noble calling, but let's agree that being that, does not mean you should transform and live your life as if - being Johnny's mother - was the defining moment of your life.

Usually men marry a *chic* – their version of hot and sexy, and they would all like to get home to one when they do *get home*.

So, even though married, it is important that you remain a *chic* for your man's sake. His *chic*. A man doesn't want to get home to a *mamma*. If your man needs a *mamma* he would go back to his father's house. It is critical for a *Married Woman* to stay a *chic* for as long as it is possible. I like the attitude of Lillian Carter who said (At age 85) "Sure I'm for helping the elderly. I'm going to be old myself someday."

I have seen young old women and I've also seen old young women. It's all in the power of your choice. One thing I do not envy women for, is the mount of juggling they have to do in one incarnation. Once married, a woman must become a mother but still a wife, even a babe. Three roles, one person.

The sad thing is most women settle for the easiest of these things — *being a mamma*. When your man comes back home he wants to see the *chic* that swept him off his feet, not a *mamma*.

Please be a good mamma without taking the traditional shape and form. Stay in your lane – you are still his baby, sugar, lover.

Also do not allow your husband to begin calling you by your children's names - the *mama-kaSibongile* stuff is not on.

In the beginning he called you 'baby, sugar, love, princess' and all the sobriquets of endearment, and it felt good. Insist on being called right, and do not by way of lifestyle give your man an option to call you somebody's mother.

While you are at it, loose that pantyhose that you put on your head when you sleep. Find a sexier way to protect your hair. With that material, you are not only confusing your husband, you are confusing the poor pantyhose too. A move from the behind to the top — is that intended as a promotion or just some nasty affirmative action?

I told a friend I was visiting about the pantyhose thing, and she got very defensive. She said that the pantyhose was simply used because it was best for the purpose. Granted it is the bomb, but remember who I am.

Moss Mashamaite, your husband on behalf of your husband, telling you things he wouldn't tell you, because men have not as yet invented the language nor the software to communicate certain sensitive things to their women. Or it could be that he is simply afraid to tell you lest you respond in a manner he did not expect nor intend.

Your man will never be able to tell you the stuff I am about to unleash on you. If your man discovers that you are at war with the crocodile, and therefore have sworn that you will be scarce at the fountain of H_2O, he will never be able to tell you.

I am talking here about a woman who is into minimum baths. How does a man tell his woman that she's got a flavour or that her armpits seem to be developing bread mould and live to tell it?

My point is, getting married is not a retirement from sexy. Just because you got your man, doesn't mean you have arrived.

Stay Sexy. Stay Foxy.

Marriage is a journey and getting married is just the beginning.

The beginning of an awesome journey that can turn awful with the throw of a dice, if you do not attend to detail. Every detail. Sexy *mamma*, foxy *mamma* - that's the way to go.

A *mamma* drove your man from his father's house and another *mamma* may just be about do the same.

I was talking to a young lady – betrothed - and we were talking about hair. Although I am not that in touch with my feminine side, I do often take my time and talk hair, nails and weight with women. That's called being a charmer.

'I wish I could just cut my hair and go bald.' She said

'Why?' I asked, my eyes gleaming with curiosity.

'I am just tired of my hair,' she answered.

'After I get married I want to shave it all off,' she continued.

I asked 'Why', and she saw the look on my face and knew exactly that she had said too much.

In other words, she was saying, 'I will groom my hair and take pains to look good until I impress a man enough for him to marry me.'

Then I will shave and look like my grandmother who is eighty-two. For *Pantsy*, hard luck! The marriage papers say, 'till death do us part.' Why should I look good anymore, I've got me *Pantsy*.

My advice to you if you've got that kind of attitude is that your husband might soon find his way to Skuurlik if you are not careful. There he will find somebody who knows just what a man wants.

Somebody who has not signed any papers and therefore is not on contract. Knowing that she is not contracted, she understands that being in the books of this man is totally on a performance only basis. She will therefore do all that has to be done, look better every day and retire the pantyhose from the odd job.

Trick and Tips from the 'Other' woman

I've got a naughty streak and I am sure you know that already. Years back, I interviewed a couple of women I knew who had relationships with married men.

Some of them were my colleagues and some were people I just knew. Of course I did tell them I was interviewing them. I asked the right questions and tongues got wagging. From that prime research I developed a series of short sermons that I used in my teaching and counselling sessions with women.

The series was entitled — "Love Tips from The Other Woman." The funny thing is, one of the ladies I interviewed said she would not get married because she loves to be the other woman.

I asked why, and she said, 'Women lose the fascination of their men when they get married, and the other woman becomes the fascination for the married man.' She said, she wanted to be a fascination forever.

I asked her how she keeps the thrill going. She told me most of the things I am writing about now. I asked her how she knew all these things and she said, 'Other than spying on her competition, most married men tell the other woman all the things they don't like about their wives and other woman takes her cue from those complaints, and then does everything right."

The biology of your Sexuality

I've seen beautiful women change and look like old bags while still young as soon as they get married. After the first child it gets worse, and while I know it's difficult keeping up with n a new addition to the human family enjoined to your already hectic life, you still must enhance your profile.

There is no excuse for tits hanging around enjoying an eternal moment with gravity. Do not mistake your breasts for little Johnny's canteen. Little Johnny will suck the life out of those breasts, and a year later he wants to eat Nando's just like everybody else. Now those tits must go back to their rightful owner.

So don't dangle them around like they were some cheap polony from Marabastad in downtown Pretoria. Those tits are your man's tits and with men often being as narrow minded as we are, them tits might just be the single most important thing that decided the diamond ring be put on your finger and not the *other* woman.

Don't get me wrong, nature has a way of working against your biology, but don't kill the goose that laid the golden egg. Dangling is not healthy for your marriage nor your man's sexuality. The same way you use makeup to cover up blemishes, keep it intact.

As man we can be stupid sometimes, but our minds function like that. Back in the day, African men never used to regard the breast as a sensual and sexual organ – but times have changed. Our minds have been colonized by the images of Halle Berry, Jennet Jackson, Tyra Banks, Naomi Campbell and many more I cannot count.

We have been thoroughly colonized, and now the breast has been put back on the menu, both as a starter and the main. The woman who used to whip the tits in the bus to give little Johnny the nurturing suckle, is a distant and rural memory.

Let us not behave like she is a present reality.

That woman is not even our mother, maybe our grandmother. Dangling breasts like they were little Johnny's pantry all over the house, with your man and little Johnny watching, could be traumatic to the male psyche.

And sex being primarily in the mind, you could be demolishing your own sexuality with every dangling act.

Man's Happy Thoughts and Happy Endings

Men's sexual imaginations are much lower than women's.

Naturally they are more imaginative with a body they have never seen, so it is important that you show him bodies he has not seen in you.

While I am on this one I would like to advise African women not to try to make their husbands be like white men. They might be neighbours and friends, but our cultures are still very different.

Let me tell you a story.

A guy I know who is a sophisticated, suburban, upper middle class fellow, was persuaded by his upper middle class wife, to go with her to the maternity ward where she would be giving birth to their little one.

He did as he was told, and he saw a baby coming out of the happy hole with his African eyes. It was like a live horror movie.

The sight of it traumatized him such that the experience landed him on Floor Eleven of Louis Pasteur Building in Pretoria.

Those who live in Pretoria know that is the psychiatric ward.

Since then has never been able to approach the happy hole ever again. Every time he saw it, his mind went back to the day when it was dilated and a human head emerging out of it.

They paid a lot of money in therapy but the marriage still ended up in divorce.

What the woman did not understand when she persuaded her man to the maternity ward, was that the African man is not wired like that.

He simply does not have the software of the European man.

He is a lover but only an African lover.

Being a Mamma — The Social Angle

Up to this point my input on being a *mamma* was mostly physical, but there is a social angle to being a *mamma*. In marital therapy sessions I have observed that women who mother their husbands end up taking away their *'in-charge-ness'*. Not knowing that this is where the male sexuality emanates from. The act of mothering does not only emasculate the man but it also *de-sexualises* the woman the mind and the eyes of the man. You get to become like their mothers, and men do not get aroused by anything that reminds them of their mothers.

Women sometimes marry men that are not their intellectual equals, and deeper into the relationship they decide they must take over from their men in the intellectual department. Unfortunately, it's too late at this stage of your relationship for me to help you.

In my book 'Ten Stupid Things Single People Say and Do' I address this in the subtitle, 'Choosing A Partner Outside of Your Species.'

To advise you on your choice of man now is not going to help – you, me or anyone. The damage was done a long time ago.

All I can say to you now is, if you have married someone you think needs motherly support, you are in trouble. You must know that there are many ways out of that dilemma, but mothering your husband is not one of them.

If you order your man around like he is a child, soon enough he becomes the child and you become the adult in the relationship.

This could even go to the bedroom where you, the Commander General would be commanding your foot soldier what to do saying things like - attention! Missionary position; Salute! Now do the doggy style.

Then later on, 'It is now time to hit it sideways!'

Poor *Pantsy* can do this for a little while, but sooner or later his maleness will tire from the routine, and he will begin to bring a shrimp to the bedroom instead of a bone, or he will find someone out there in Skuurlik who will let him be the man.

It's the man's turn to say 'I have a headache.' And you say, 'get some Grandpa.' And he says, 'I already have a grandma, what do I need a grandpa for.'

Women naturally have a brain to run things and pretend that it is the man in charge and make him believe so too.

Have you ever heard this one; 'I am the man in this house and everything that my wife wants will be done.' That to me is the diplomatic way out of the dilemma of a man having married a woman who is his intellectual superior.

And that does not need mothering.

I have interviewed a lot of men informally and formally; sometimes they knew I was interviewing them and sometimes they didn't because I was just striking conversation.

Out of those sessions I have come to know that a great number of men are terrified of their wives.

Even the ones who pretend to be.

A man sometimes misses his mother and would like to visit, but as soon as he becomes a man he does not want to go home to his mother — period.

So when you become a *mamma* you make it extremely difficult for the man to be *the man*. You take away his sense of independence and control. You turn him into a child again.

I've seen a lot of men report lots of stupid things to their wives like they were little children, and the control freaks enjoying the moment all the way.

It's a sad thing and it must be discouraged.

As much as we are all here on earth because our mothers slept with some guy — our biological father, we don't want to imagine our mothers doing the act.

Sex is in the mind and sexually speaking what you can't imagine you can't experience. So becoming a *mamma* to your man will injure his responses to you as a woman. And most man would rather be with the *chic* - hopefully not from *Skuurlik* or God forbid *Dunusa*.

Being a Mamma — The Emasculation of Men

I know a guy who got drunk as hell and engaged himself in a brawl and a fist fight that turned into some karate ass kicking. They kicked his behind and his beneath so hard that one of his little marbles shot up and disappeared into his body cavity.

He went for weeks with only one marble - I guess the other marble had decided on absenteeism with very good reasons. This is a metaphor for the emasculated male. One migrated marble and one in place, huffing and puffing in this *sexathon* we call life.

The submissive type of man is still a man and he is still your husband. He is a grown up too, you wouldn't have married him if he wasn't. It is important to treat him well and be a wife instead of a mother. It is a woman's job to fan the flames of desire in her man's heart. The captive man has no desire in him - it is the free man who does.

The thing that women do, retiring from being *chics* to being mothers and sexless creatures of the crib, is what mostly keeps the bed of marriage icy.

Yes, that cold.

It's what keeps *Skuurlik* - or *Dunusa* for that matter- in business. Samuel Taylor Coleridge says:

"Where the true love burns, Desire is love's pure flame,
It is the reflex of our earthly frame,
That takes its meaning from the nobler part,
And but translates the language of the heart."

Something attracted your man to you. There were still more than three billion people of the female species here on earth, and your man picked you. If you know what it is that attracted him to you, then you are a lucky woman because you know where the trigger to your marital wellbeing is.

Remember that which attracted your man to you is mostly physical. You might have a good heart, you might be daring, but those are your invisible attributes. Don't give them up on those sexy attributes.

Do not give sexy up until you are eighty-eight and a half, if you ever get there – even then, keep it sexy you never know some young blood is looking for collectibles and you might just be the spark the flames his fire. But if you are not interested in Ben 10s, at that age, you may as well be dead anyway. Even if he is still alive, he would still be dead to physical parts that attracted him to you.

Then you can bring on the pantyhose from retirement to cover up your gray hair if you have any left, or shave your head until it shines like Isaac Hayes. At that time, you know it wouldn't destroy your sex life.

Remember the competition

Most women don't like to see their men reading girlie magazines and I don't mean Playboy and some triple X stuff, I mean any magazine with sexy women in it.

The message is, 'I don't want to see you looking at sexy women - am I not enough?' Or it is, 'I don't want you looking at sexy women, I want you to be looking at this *mamma*.' Instead of pitching at the level of the foxy girlie, women chose to persecute their men and play the role of policeman in their man's life.

Being a woman and a wife is already a hectic occupation, now if you add 'top cop' to your CV, it just gets worse for you. You might at this point go defensive and say, 'But I am sure my man would also not like to see me looking at a man with a six pack in Men's Health magazine.' Or you could say, "it's unfair — the only six pack my man knows is that of Castle Lager. How can he expect me to be a foxy mamma?" Life is unfair. Deal with it! The man without a six pack still needs a woman who looks good and there are many women who look mighty good who will fall for him still. Haven't you heard the song, "It's Raining Men," has been banned?

Take care of your man, the good ones are either taken or extinct

It is not raining men. It's never rained men.

There is a global shortage of men.

Let me break it down for you – there are not too many times in recorded history when men outnumbered. The one-time man outnumbered women was in the Garden of Eden.

Eve, Adam, Cain and Abel.

Cane took it upon himself to reduce the ratio from 3:1 down to 2:1. And the one in this ratio was his mamma - all in one angry moment.

The only other time in recorded history was in Egypt during the days of Moses, Pharaoh killed every Israeli male child born - only Moses survived – so we are told.

During the time of the birth of Jesus, Herod killed every male child born. There are more girls born than boys and on top of that boys have a higher infant mortality rate.

After all that, who goes to war? Who works in the mines?

Need I say more?

Men are indeed a species threatened with extinction.

Look after yours.

Being a Mamma — Hygiene and Sex

Like I said earlier, the $H_2 0$ affairs in your relationship should be left to me. I want to take this topic head on right now. The Holy Book says, 'love your neighbour.'

I say before you even love your neighbour, love *thy* water. I am not talking about bathing; I am talking about being in love with water.

Water has many purposes in a woman's life.

Most men have a problem with a woman who takes a bath once a day – in the morning and in the evening thinks she is ready to make love to her man. For me, love making is derived from the book of Genesis 3 - "And Adam knew his wife."

I would like at this stage to borrow Dan Brown's lingo from "The Da Vinci Code" and call the female sexual nerve center, the rose.

Cunnilingus is a must and the rose is an internal organ just like the mouth. The mouth speaks and tells lies all day long and therefore can ventilate better than the rose. So if you want your rose eaten, which does not only enhance pleasure during the act of love making, but also lifts up the female ego, you must wash it thoroughly. Douche when there is need and attend to it with diligence.

This includes all things that you need licked and eaten. In the world of Sigmund Freud, we have talked so much of the male ego we have almost forgotten that there is to some extant, a female ego.

The male ego is directly tied to a man's sexual tools, his bank account and all things male - like provision of food, shelter and security for the family.

The female ego on the other hand is tied to things like beauty, hygiene, cleanliness, even preparation of food, sex, girth, and etc.

Actually the female ego is rather detailed. That is why women need more compliments than men.

A man must say to his woman, 'the food was delicious,' 'your ass looks good,' 'you made mighty good love to me,' 'the house is clean,' 'you smell like a garden of roses' (not Dan Brown's rose of course) etc. And then the woman can light up the house with female energy.

A woman who washes once a day is definitely damaging her sexual life. I know that in our country there are cultures that believe that one shouldn't wash the rose too often, for with too much washing, you may also wash away the taste.

I declare that backwards in the most Stone Age term of the Word.

So a woman must wash at least twice a day as a routine.

There is nothing like a bad flavour to destroy the sex appetite.

I knew a guy once, who was pursuing one of the finest women I had ever seen.

She had it all, the ass - ATM (African Trade Marks), the cleavage, the legs, and the face — she was a complete specimen of woman. He ultimately got the woman for a girlfriend and he excitedly told me about his conquest.

He told me how he got her but he will never get to sleep with her again. I asked him 'Why'. And he said, 'Whatever chemical engineering is going on down there, somebody must be trying to concoct weapons for biological warfare.'

Hygiene is critical

A woman who wears her inner clothes more than once, hoping that her husband is suffering from severe sinusitis is simply ignorant – and the right word is STUPID.

I suspect men who do not eat the rose for sexual inadequacy and lack of imagination, but I equally suspect men who eat the unwashed rose — I fear that such a person could eat anything.

If your man likes to eat it, wash it clean.

Let it be such that if he eats it, he will eat the spices of love, not yesterday's residual others.

The man who eats the rose is a King, treat him like that.

This is especially true for the African man because the white man was raised to eat the rose. They even put chocolate, ice cream and whipped cream on it; and everything just becomes a sex cuisine.

Being a mamma means not thinking of yourself in a sexual way.

You wake up in your pyjamas and do domestic work and when your husband comes back home you haven't changed the morning look.

My suggestion about minimum bathing times is — men — external organs, therefore minimum once a day in winter, minimum twice in hot weather. Women — internal organs, therefore minimum baths — twice in winter and twice or more in summer, depending on the weather and the occupation.

There are no maximum bathing times, but please do not spend twenty-four hours in water. One thing that has forever baffled me is why fish stink so much – could it be that they spend all day in water. I don't know, I am not a marine biologist. Neither is your man – at least he shouldn't be forced to be.

Dance like no one is watching

Mammas are more worried about bathing their kids and cleaning their houses than they worry about bathing themselves. The tragedy in that is, even clean *mammas* (as in great housekeepers) could easily become dirty *mammas*.

Being a mamma might also mean - 'Now that I am a *mamma* I am going to have sex like my kids are watching.'

Doggy style? – Noooo!

It might also mean you have a child like Snoop Dogg, which could be tragic.

You might be a pastor, which makes you a pastor's wife so you thing, 'Doggy style might just make us look cheap and horny.'

'Let us settle for more dignified positions — what about missionary, it's even biblical, even though I might not be able to prove it.'

I have always wondered why the man on top sexual pose is called the missionary position. The missionary position is all about having sex like God is watching. Personally I don't think that the first man made love to the first woman like God was watching, because they didn't have a bed and Adam first observed sex from animals.

In the sex department very few animals are missionaries.

Let's face it, you charmed your man into marrying you, the attraction was mostly and initially physical. The same thing that drew him to you must keep him with you, he should still keep coming for more. Every woman dreams of growing old with their man, but unfortunately most men watch their women grow old beside them.

Being a Mamma — The Beautiful Thing About Beauty

Beauty is a gift from God but it is also an effort, especially as you grow older. I have been around for a long time and I have never really seen an ugly woman. I have seen women who neglected themselves and women who looked after themselves.

I have seen women who knew what worked for them and women who were clueless, but an ugly woman I have never really spied. And it is important to be beautiful for you, before it's for anybody else, even your man. When you embark on losing weight it should be for you and that way it is sustainable.

I have also realised that beauty is lodged sometimes in how you dress yourself up and how you carry yourself. In this regard I will venture to say I've never seen an ugly well-dressed person, and I mean well dressed for themselves. I am not a reality TV freak, but I have enjoyed some really interesting shows, especially the make-over shows, and there is one thing that make-over shows reveal.

They reveal that there is no ugly person in this world. There are those who look good and those who need make-overs.

I am an average looking guy myself, but you should see me in an Armani suit, even I look good. I believe it was Mark Twain who said "Clothes make the man, and the naked man has no influence in this world."

Always choose Happiness

Someone asked me what I think about extreme make-overs like plastic surgery, boob jobs, etc.

My answer was, 'firstly, blame society.' Society and family and parents can be so hard on your nose that one day when you have a little change, you could buy yourself a brand new face. They can call you plain Jane until you buy boobs or looks.

Secondly, we are all here on earth to be happy, amongst other things.

If everything Abraham Maslow could teach you on self-actualization does not help you be happy with who you are, and a plastic surgeon promises to fix it with the scalpel. And when he is through you are happier, I say I vote for happiness any day.

Will God be mad at you?

I don't think He'll be mad at you just as BMW Corporation will never be mad at a person who pimps an M3.

Besides, his pronouncement has been made long ago. "Dust thou art and to dust thou shalt return!"

In the case of Michael Jackson, he might have to rephrase; "Plastic thou art and to plastic thou shalt return."

Same difference!

As Henry David Thoreau emphasized, when He (God) said those words - He was not talking of the soul, but the body.

Do you think God doesn't know Michael Jackson anymore?

I'm pretty sure He does.

I bet you He knows him well and he liked him.

Besides, if it was not for plastic surgery, the phenomenon and the legend of Michael Jackson would not have quite come upon us as it has.

I tell you what, every science has given us its greatest creation and I dare say, plastic surgery gave the World Michael Jackson and we should be grateful for it.

Was it King Solomon who said, "Charm is deceitful and beauty is vain, but the woman who fears the Lord is to be praised!"

I will tell you this, he was the greatest charmer of them all.

He wrote a complete book to charm one black woman, one of his thousand wives, and he surrounded himself with beauty and beauties. So he did not practice what he preached and we should dismiss him with Barry White's famous song "Practice what you preach."

On a serious note though, it is my opinion that King Solomon was prioritizing in that statement.

In essence, he was saying, 'Be charming', 'Be beautiful' and 'Fear the Lord', but in this order:

>> Fear the Lord and

>> Practice charm and

>> Make it a point that you are a dazzling beauty on a daily basis, and then you are the man - as in, the Woman.

Making The Right Investments

Maybe, at this stage I should mention dental hygiene. Nothing turns a man off like stale breath.

I know most men have bad habits like smoking and drinking which most women do not have, but somehow women have survived with men whose mouths smelled like sewers.

For this I am led to believe women run on a different software. I will go on a limb and accept that this software (SBT 3.0 or Stale Breath Tolerance 3.0) was sold by Microsoft to an exclusively female clientele.

Men do not possess that software.

Even stinking breath men.

So as a woman, you must not only brush your teeth in the morning and before you sleep, but if you do not have the software to tolerate bad breath, make *double* tooth brushing and daily flossing a habit and encourage your entire family to do so, including your man. It will help you a lot.

Convince all your children that gingivitis is a deadly disease.

Then you tell your man that you read in a health magazine that according to a study made in the U.K. it was discovered that gingivitis reduces libido in men over the age of '*however old you husband is*'. And that the study recommended that men ought to brush their teeth at least three times a day.

Remember kissing and oral works are at least fifty percent of romance. I personally believe that every family should invest in various portfolios financially, but never forget to invest in a company called Stimorol – or any of its competitors with menthol sweets and gum – Halls, etc.

Gum that helps your breath is critical.

You must always have some gum when you are not sure of your oral ambiance.

Remember that kissing is uptown window shopping for downtown purchasing.

Becoming a Mamma — The Kids Factor

Your children were not born to become your first love?

As soon as they have children most women begin to beam their love on the kids in such a manner the husband begins to fade away in the darkness of a *mis-focussed* beam.

Even if I have to say so myself, this is wrong.

The love for your children should be full without depleting the main source. When you show partiality between children and their father, you are doing nobody a favour, not even the children.

You should know that the most beautiful thing for your children to see is mommy and daddy in love. That is the greatest way to love your kids. Obviously they would like to compete with that, but usually they don't mind losing to their father. Your romance should therefore not die a slow death with your newly born baby. Do not become a *mamma* until there is no more lover in you.

This is the order — first a lover, then a wife and then a mommy.

The mommy role shouldn't take all the energy because it is a supplemented role. There is always daddy and therefore there should be enough love for the children from both of you.

Becoming a Mamma- The Development of Self

The greatest problem in becoming a *mamma* to the exclusion of all things you could become, means that most women let their lives atrophy and no longer develop their gifts and discontinue further learning efforts.

I have heard plenty women say, 'I used to play the piano.'

And you ask, 'What happened?'

The answer goes, 'I got married.'

When did married and buried become synonyms?

All healthy men would like to build their lives around growing beings. You enjoy seeing your children grow and you enjoy seeing your wife grow. I know there are those who are threatened by such developments. I have one word for those — stupid!

You've got to develop yourself intellectually even financially as an independent being. Remember no matter how hard you work on your marriage, it could end up in divorce, or still, you could be widowed.

The odds are against you

In her book, 'Rich Woman' - Kim Kiyosaki states, "47% of women over the age of 50 are single, 50% of marriages end in divorce. In the first year after divorce a woman's standard of living drops by an average of 73%. Of the elderly living in poverty, 3 out of 4 are women — and 80% of them were not poor when their husbands were alive. Nearly 7 out of 10 women will at some time live in poverty."

These are scary statistics, but it's reality and I will tell you why?

It's because married women make a profession out of becoming *mammas* and leave the rest of their lives and personal development aside, because they have an eternal lover in their husbands.

Most businesses I have observed when I was growing up, which were mostly retail and wholesale shops, would plummet to the ground when the man dies. Almost 9 out of 10 of them because it somehow never occurred to the woman that this courageous businessman of hers may not be there forever.

Therefore, she does not need to develop the very skill that is putting bread on their table.

They just watch from a distance and become little Johnny's mother and the village snob.

If that is your attitude, you better be very nice to the people of the community because one day you will be begging for bread from them.

In 'Rich Woman', Kim Kiyosaki deals with stupid things married women do where finances are concerned, and she has countless examples of such situations.

Situations where women lacked vision and anticipation and only celebrated the present joy of the bliss of matrimony.

Didn't help that most of the fairy tales they ever read were suffixed with "... and they lived happily ever after."

I am talking here about abandoning the vital facets of your life just because some *dude* put a gold and diamond ring on your finger.

You as a woman must understand that you are a spirit that lives in a body and a god in your own right, simply inhabiting a female body. You are here on a divine mission of your own and you will have to account to God for your own separate life.

When you get married, none of the things I just mentioned change. Becoming somebody's wife or another's mate does not exonerate you from the calling that God has bestowed upon you at birth.

Remember yourself

Let me say this harshly so you may never forget it, you are not a womb-man, you are a woman. You are not all about giving birth and nurturing.

Look, motherhood and *wife-hood* in themselves are great and noble occupations, but they both involve other people, your husband and your children.

It is you becoming something for other people.

Let's not forget a little selfishness here.

You were born alone and in most cases you will die alone.

You will come before God's accounting throne alone and will have to give an individual account of what you did with your life.

Your husband might be there forever or he might leave you for a younger woman, hell even for a younger man these days.

Your children will leave you one day unless you have given birth to live-at-home-morons. So in short, in the course of your life, remember, the cover on your body might be ripped off one way or another and then you will realise that abandoning your life for a husband and children was not worth it.

You are responsible for your personal growth, your individual financial growth, your spiritual growth and the growth of every plant and flower in the garden of your life.

Sitting down on the grandstands and becoming your children's cheerleader and your husband's number one fan, is dangerous for your health.

Cheer you must.

And a fan you should be.

But you must do this and still not neglect your own life.

"Having sex is like playing bridge. If you don't have a good partner, you'd better have a good hand."
 - *Woody Allen*

The woman who used to whip the tits in the bus to give little Johnny suck is a distant and rural memory. Let us not behave like she is present reality.

That woman is not even our mother, maybe our grandmother.

Dangling breasts like they were little Johnny's pantry all over the house with your man and little Johnny watching, could be traumatic to the male psyche.

And sex being primarily in the mind, you could be demolishing your own sexuality with every dangling act

Two

I Have a Headache

We all fight battles during the day in the workplace or wherever it is that you spend your time. Married men and married women, we all retreat to a place where we can either replenish our strengths or weaken each other even more. This place could be named the bedroom, the boardroom or simply the *bored*-room.

Either way, as far as influencing the events in life and the entire history of the homosapien - per square meter - this is probably the most powerful place on planet earth, second to none. Even the altar and the throne room - call it the Union Building, the White House or the Vatican even, all play second fiddle to this - on average - thirty five square meter space.

It is the Garden of Eden reincarnated where the snake, the man, the woman and their God wrestle each other for the destiny of future generations.

Sex is a very volatile subject in any relationship. I have argued earlier that it was repressed sexual energy that was possible responsible for the first murder. The first two boys, sons of the first two people had grown up and their bodies were ready to copulate and there were no females around to help them out.

The only woman known to them was their mother.

One slight misunderstanding, one moment of discontent and Cain kills his brother. It doesn't make sense.

The Grace before the Law

Before there was Moses, and before the *Law Giver* gave his commandments - the famous 'Thou Shalt Nots,' there was God.

In the garden of innocence, He localized Himself and strolled with straddling strides speaking to man, face to face.

In those days He was not as legalistic as He would later become during the days of Moses, or rather as Moses presented Him to be.

Firm he was. And whatever he wanted observed, He articulated in great eloquence but was also vehement in laying down the consequences of trespassing the law.

Nevertheless, His first commandment was not uttered in the 'Mosaic' spirit of 'the law'. It was simple, straight forward and non-judgmental. "Be fruitful and multiply and fill the earth…" He said. It thrills my very bones that God's first commandment was that human beings should copulate, and copulate hard, until they populate the earth to full capacity.

So as humans we have a divine mandate to copulate. The initial purpose was for the multiplication and the survival of the species, now it's for replenishment, with survival in view.

In medical school they teach about the survival of the species, and four things that have ensured that we as a species are still here whereas a lot of creatures have gone extinct.

I have simplified them so that they are easily remembered – let's call them the four F's.

Feed, Fight, Flight and F...

Of course I meant Fornicate for the purposes of Procreation.

We must all admit that outside of procreation the copulation, or rather *Fornication* command serves a whole lot more purposes than most people would like to admit.

Sex has many benefits:

>> It is therapeutic

>> It reduces stress

>> It is enjoyable

>> It can strengthen the bond in human relationships and again

>> It is extremely enjoyable, especially when it's done right. It might get dirty but that's because you are doing it right.

This is, of course when you are actually having sex, not just talking about it. But if you are not having it, every positive mentioned above, turns into a bitter negative.

A fly on the wall of a bedroom can tell you a lot of things great, small and nasty that's happening in bedrooms. One of the things I bet my life on, a fly on the wall having heard would be, "I have a headache!"

Down the road of any relationship women will use this excuse not to have sex with their husbands. This is such an old excuse our grandmothers used it on our grandfathers and it was passed on to our mothers who used it on our fathers. Now it has entered the female DNA.

And by the way, 'I have a headache' is not literal. It is a metaphor for many things, often a substitute of "I'm tired", "Not today honey.", "I'm not feeling like it" or "I think I'm coming down with something"

'I have a headache' is so cliché one has to be very unoriginal to use it. Yet even the most creative and original married woman uses it.

If you repeatedly use the 'I have a headache' phrase and your husband in an attempt to fight it, offers you 'Grand Pa' which works faster because it's powder, you are still married.

If he doesn't fight at all and sooner says that he is going out to hang with the boys, you are in trouble. You have probably over-stretched the 'I have a headache' franchise.

Sooner or later you will discover that the boys he hangs out with put on thongs and have breasts and they live in *Skuurlik* somewhere or most likely *Dunusa*.

Woman, beware of the man who does not put up a fight when he is denied due benevolence.

That is a red light right there.

When He Is a Headache

That you have a headache might mean a lot of things. That I understand very clearly, and wish all the men out there had the same software that I've got on this one.

It might mean the guy who wants to have your rose has been demanding everything from food to the toilet paper - two-ply *nogal* - to having his clothes ironed and you think he doesn't deserve it.

Generally, women have a higher vocabulary than men and all that is thanks to practice which makes perfect.

So, why don't you just say it?

Why don't you nicely say to your husband, 'It's a little difficult to be a washing machine, a cook, a baby sitter and a sex vending machine all in one day while your man is a newspaper-reading couch potato waiting for a moment to prowl. Why don't you help me?'

Or better still, 'Pumpkin, if you could please think for me and give me a little hand once in a while, you might just find out that when we go to bed I still have enough energy to enjoy you.'

Before I even knew what sex was, I saw Mr. Rooster chase Mother Hen for just a three second screw.

Imagine a teenage cock with a premature ejaculation problem.

He begins to run after Sister Hen and then stops to pick up some seeds with a happy face. Sister Hen doesn't even know that Brother Hen has accomplished his mission.

I want to argue that the scene I witnessed while I was young is true also for the homosapien. Like Mother Hen, the female species has forever pretended that it hates sex. The male species bought into the lie and consequently has been on the begging end of the coitus stick.

This is good for women to keep control of things, and besides, if a man opened the door of their house and they found another narrow doorway equally and widely open daily, they would run away.

Fact! As much as men love sex they do not like the type that is so captive it cannot say no. Men are incurable hunters who still do not mind hunting for the quarry they have already captured.

So women, you are in a dilemma.

It is as dangerous to say 'YES' all the time, just as much as it is dangerous to say 'NO' most of the time.

When It's Not a Headache

When it's not a headache, 'I have a headache' is destructive marital state. So let us together invent ways to heal the female headache that is not even a headache.

Sex is in the mind, so to improve your libido you must improve your psychology. A woman, more than a man, must read, see and explore her sexuality and things relating to sex.

The headache that women experience is more — a HEAD that has lost focus in the clutter of the multiplicity of things that women have to deal with on a daily basis than men - that than becomes a real headache.

It is actually a forgetfulness borne out of focusing on many other things. Women therefore often have to be reminded of sex.

They must communicate with their men in reminding ways, or they should remind themselves.

Money, Sex, Power... Oh! Sorry I meant Romance

The problem is that often women marry an unromantic dude just because he can fill a supermarket trolley with goodies with his eyes closed.

When you choose your man you must remember that you are not all stomach, you are also a sensual and sexual being. Remember it is more difficult to school a man in the erotic elements of love than a woman. Hell, the male ego is so tightly married to his sexuality you cannot touch one without messing with the other. If you came up with a new bedroom move, a man could get suspicious and wonder which school taught you that move.

That's why it's advisable that even when you pick up a revolutionary book about sex and its 'how-tos' or discover in a moment of great epiphany the Kama Sutra, you should let your spouse in on it too.

This is because sex is the most sensitive part of any relationship and change management is a critical and hectic part of any organization.

Managing Sex Dynamics

Imagine sex revolution meeting 'change management' in the organization of your home boardroom. Disaster is in the air, I promise. So, as a smart woman, you must know not only how to ration the love bed, but how and when to, all for the furtherance of the success of the family.

The great traditional problem with sex and sexuality is that in most cultures parents do not teach their children about it. Society in most cultures is simply hypocritical about sex and unfortunately most women learn about the how to's, the when to's,' and the when not to's from the streets.

They also learn from their most talkative friends, the ones who do not mind going graphic and techno-colourful about their own bedroom experiences with their husbands or anybody else. These loud mouth sisters are not really qualified except by their loud mouth, and yet; you, the undiscerning disciple might consequently get into big trouble.

I Can Do Without It for A Year

Another stupid thing that I've heard women say, sometimes within the hearing distance of their male significant other is, 'I can do without it for a year.'

I am bringing this in the fray because it has the ability to affect the department of sex in the family, just like the 'I have a headache' line.

I've heard women say they can go without *it* for a year.

This is a lie of course, and women know that.

If you really want to know for how long a woman can go without it, ask their best friend who speaks nasty stuff with them. That which she knows is the truth.

Women are just as much into sex as men are, with *undepletable* resources on top of that.

The problem with this statement, 'I Can Do Without It for A Year' and the reason I say it is stupid, is because most men don't know – with woman, most of the time, the truth is the exact opposite of what they say.

When a woman says, 'I am moving out!' And you say 'Well maybe that's what you need,' the first thing she is going to tell her best friend is, 'I told him I am moving out and he didn't even try to stop me.' Because men don't know this, most of them believe that women are half saints when it comes to sex.

You and I know that women are just as nasty, because all the nasty things men do, they do with women – except obviously for the few who choose not to.

Question is, where do you draw the line?

The only difference between men and women and the issue of sex is that to women sex is power and to men, a weakness.

Sex and the Thrill of the Chase

Women pretend to not like it because that gives them power. As long as your man thinks that it is a laborious exercise to you, he is going to have to beg for it. Besides, if your man came home and found you every day putting on your nicely laundered, sta-softened and creaselessly ironed birthday suit, saying, 'Take me!' Most men – at least the ones I know - would run for their lives.

When I was still single and a young Pastor, a man in my church came to my house, in fact fled to my house and told me he was running away from home because his pregnant wife was insatiable.

She just wanted sex and more sex.

I couldn't get it.

I was young, celibate and horny as a goat, just holding my breath in the name of the Lord Jesus Christ and here was a man running away from pleasure.

The last Psychology book I read had said that life was a constant flight from pain to pleasure, and here was some fool running away from pleasure. I didn't have the software then to understand what was going on. I was so tempted to offer my non-existent gigolo services as part of my pastoral duties.

My little memory of sex or 'almost sex' was dealt a blow.

Sexual Domination

Man was created by nature to be more powerful than woman, physically at least. But God being judicious and abundant in humour gave the woman sexuality for the balance of power between the sexes. And indeed, women have used their sexuality to get anything from favours to kingdoms.

The greatest of women will use this God-given power to build successful and happy homes and by extension, societies.

'I have a headache' is a valid assertion. You might just have a headache; your man might be a headache or you might just be wanting to show the man who the Queen is.

So 'I have a headache' is a power game, a potent weapon in the traditional arsenal of the Tribe of Eve.

Talking about Eve, most people think that she was not a virgin when Adam got to love her in the grass. They misinterpret Genesis Chapter 3 to mean that the snake was the woman's first lover.

I think that is sick and absurd.

The fruit in the Garden of Eden was plain fruit and the sexuality of the first woman was the preserve of the first man, period.

I would like you as a woman at least to give respect to the first woman by buying into my argument before we even continue on this road.

I often wonder what our fore-mothers - the world is so chauvinistic I might even be the first person on planet earth to ever use the word fore-mother - had as an excuse for not having sex with our fore-fathers, the beasts who dominated all the way and even invented the missionary position, just to make sure it's clear who the man was.

Could they ever say 'I have a headache' even if they did'?

I think not.

That is why the world is so overpopulated with stupid people.

The man wasn't listening so a non-listening stupid DNA was passed on.

The Restoration of the Bedroom

Contrary to popular belief about sex and its *physical-ness*, it is perhaps the most spiritual thing any two people can ever engage in.

No wonder it is the central theme of prohibition in most religions or even the central theme of worship in some.

Right or wrong, sex is the only way - outside of science - that two people can bring another human being on planet earth - a divine being at that. So no book about the most important and most primary human relationship — marriage, can boast to be worth its salt or could ever be complete without addressing this subject. The bedroom is the temple of human worship where two people - this beyond even the physical - become one flesh. The bed is the shrine and sex is an act and a form of worship.

Using the worship analogy, when you go to the temple to worship you forget about yourself and lavish attention, adoration and adulation on the object of your worship.

This does not mean you are not going to get due benefit. In fact, the more you focus on the other, the more the splendour of the transference to you. If two people went into the temple of sex both being of the same mind — this mind I am trying to inculcate, the bedroom would be turned into a place where two people could connect at levels that transcend physical bliss as it is known.

Since this is not a book about sex I do not want to be more explicit, I believe you do catch my drift.

Finding Sexual Healing

Instead of 'I have a headache' therefore I can't do it. When the bedroom has been restored as a temple of erotic worship the woman would say rather, 'I have a headache, let's go to the bedroom.'

Marvin Gaye sang a song - 'Sexual Healing'. A beautiful song that was not well received by naive religious minds. I most certainly regard that song as an anthem of erotic love.

Finding Marital Bliss

As a woman, it is within your province and your interest to restore your bedroom to its honeymooned splendour. The bedroom is your powerhouse, your military base in the battle marital bliss.

The power of sex in a marriage was given to the woman not the man. Sex is your power-base in your relationship.

History is resplendent with the archetypes of sexual prowess who literally became female goddesses and ran kingdoms and empires. Women like Samson's Delilah, Bathsheba's David, Julius Caesar and Mark Anthony's Cleopatra. Need I say J.F. Kennedy's Marilyn Monroe? I am mentioning these Women only to demonstrate my point, not for any other purposes.

You're the goddess of your Sex Temple

As the goddess of the sex temple in your home, you are responsible for the interior decor, the drapery, the dress code or 'undress codex.'

You are responsible for choosing the bed and the bedding, the flowers and paintings that will adorn your temple, and you've got to be meticulous. Every little detail matters.

I have seen bedrooms that just say — tired. They do not only reflect the sex life of the inhabitants but in many ways also determine it.

The main bedroom is the first room of the house. If you have money to spend you must begin here. Unfortunately for most people, the main bedroom takes the back seat because your visitors don't get to see it. This is a gross mistake, your visitors don't stay in your house long enough to affect and determine where and how money should be prioritized in it.

A woman who would invest time and money to learn some more of the arts of relaxation and administering therapy and warmth with her hands, and scents and salts, will do much better as a goddess than the one who would simply say, 'I don't know how to do that. Do I look Chinese?'

And by the way, while we are at that. Can we leave the Chinese people alone just once? Everywhere I go I hear, Chinese, Chinese, Chinese. Enough!

I've seen book titles that were very encouraging of bedroom frolics with titles like, "How to be a bitch to your man," or "Being a bitch in the bedroom" and while I sympathize with their enthusiasm, I must say that there is a huge difference between a bitch and a goddess.

The women I am referring to are not bitches, they were goddesses. There is something cheap about a bitch, and somehow a bitch is blind to the spirituality and other aspects of lovemaking.

After sex, the bitch retires. Not a goddess, with a goddess, what happens before, during and after sex, all fall within the province of her sovereignty.

The bedroom is her throne and she never, ever abdicates her position for whatever reason.

To spell out the difference here I will take you to ancient Greece through one of Homer's Iliad's or poems about the goddess of love Aphrodite, the root name from which we derive our English name - aphrodisiac.

As you would know, an aphrodisiac will turn a lame duck man into a raging tiger in the bedroom. It works better than the seduction of an exotic dancer.

It seems to come from within and without, all at the same time.

Enter Homer

I will sing of stately Aphrodite,
gold-crowned and beautiful,
whose dominion is the walled cities of all sea-set Cyprus.
there the moist breath of the western wind,
wafted her over the waves
of the loud-moaning sea in soft foam,
and there the gold-filleted hours
welcomed her joyously.

They clothed her with heavenly garments
on her head they put a fine,
well- Wrought crown of gold,
and in her pierced ears
they hung ornaments of orichalc
and precious gold,
and adorned her with golden necklaces
over her soft neck and snow-white breasts,
jewels which the gold-filleted hours wear themselves
whenever they go to their father's house
to join the lovely dances of the gods.

And when they had fully decked her,
they brought her to the gods,
who welcomed her when they saw her,
giving her their hands.
Each one of them prayed that he might lead her home
to be his wedded Wife,
so greatly were they amazed at the amazed
at the beauty of violet-crowned Cytherea.

Let's face it, many a woman has found out that the bedroom is a bit more complicated and sophisticated than a bitch can handle. It is beauty and splendour and a hint of seduction that can transform the bedroom into a temple. Nasty is good, but nasty is just part of a repertoire. It's an act that is only meaningful within an elaborate play. Sadly, the married woman is nobody's student. Society has decided long ago that sex and its performances are some of the arts that you are going to have to learn for yourself.

Having pastored for many years and having observed the evolution of this generation, I insist that we are evolving faster than our ability to handle some of the intricacies of our existence. Meaning, we are going to have to teach our children some of the things that were formerly taboo.

Admittedly, the man on the other hand, needs the same rigorous education to balance the equation. My approach must never be determined in isolation. Everything that I postulate and teach in the woman book I reiterate with even greater aggression to men.

As you go through this book you must never at any given time, think that I am playing for the men's team and therefore I am trying to tame the women's team.

In this game it would please you to know that I am not a player, but a referee or maybe even somewhat of a coach. My job is to observe and enforce the rules for the purposes of fair play, or help your improve your skill in the ever changing game of marital sex play. Let me retire Homer and close this thought with one of my own.

The Bedroom Supreme

Much as would like to dazzle in speech
And hide my thoughts and mind in words
I still want to paint a picture as clear
For all and sundry too see
So none shall be found who shall disrespect
the power of the bedroom supreme
Just thirty five square meters about
Yet the most powerful seat on planet dust
Not the Vatican, nor the Union Building
Nor the White House nor the altar
Has caused so much revolution
So much revolt and so much havoc
As the bedroom supreme

The headquarters of the world?
Not the United Nations so divided
Or the seat of government
Of the Pre-eminent superpower of the day
Any day, things that change all the time
But a place that has stayed constant
The mighty bedroom supreme

Let us travel our minds to days of yore
Ere the revolution France was ruled
By a King with a large jaw
And a Queen who loved shoes
From her power seat the bedroom supreme
Mary Antoinette with her many shoes
Calling the shots from under the silk

While Louis with a boisterous tone of wine
Reverberated the status quo and the protocol
Pretending that the words were all his own
When he simply provided the tone
While the lungs all belonged to Mary with the shoes
Who called the shots from her power-base
The mighty bedroom supreme
The story continues throughout the ages
The battle is not for those with might

But for those with sight
The sight to see not the weapons of war
But the weapons endowed upon them
As nature pleased, and use them
To win the battle of the ages
The battle that leads to total peace and serenity

"What Women Want - to be loved, to be listened to, to be desired, to be respected, to be needed, to be trusted, and sometimes, just to be held. What Men Want - Tickets for the world series."

 - *Dave Berry*

Three

WENA LE SOKHANYANA YE YA GAGO

For those who do not speak the Sotho languages of Southern Africa, this title *'Wena Le Sokhanyana Ye Ya gago'* means, 'You and Your Stupid Soccer.'

I picked this out from a television advertisement where a woman was very pissed off about something her man did not do.

This he would have done had it not been for the stupid soccer game. She said this in the presence of his friends. However, because soccer is really stupid, as in beyond passion, the man was not hurt by the remark. The beautiful game was on course and all of his emotions including anything from love to hate and anger were focused on what was going on, on the telly.

It made me think though.

Suddenly the woman had switched into adult mode. She was the adult and the husband was the child who was doing childish things, and he was getting treatment that was commensurate with his behaviour according the to the woman.

That, in the presence of everybody else. It made a good advertisement, but she made a terrible wife. Especially because the husband would still somewhat continue doing what he was doing anyway.

Men do take abuse where their favourite sport is concerned, but is it really necessary? Should they go to Beijing just like women did, to get a little sensitivity coming their way?

Remember, everybody has their Achilles' heel. Women have shopping and all the other female things that you might want your man to give you support on.

An English adage goes — those who live in glass houses should not throw stones. Girl, you live in a glass house and you are throwing stones the size of soccer balls at your man's house — a house within your house.

Men are creatures with balls and a woman needs, above all else, to be able to handle her man's balls skilfully. Get off your perverted horse and get on the same page with me.

The balls I am talking about are bigger balls than you are thinking. Football, rugby, cricket, tennis, even the grand prix — I am talking about your man's sports. Most men love sports. Those who don't love sports, love things you would wish they rather loved sports if you knew what is good for you.

Know your Man's Balls

When my daughter was young, around the age of 10 years, every chance I got, I took her to the stadium to watch a game of soccer. In my opinion, as a man, that is how to raise a girl-child, and besides, what's more important is that we got to bond.

I wanted the sport to grow on her so that when she grows up, she would have one up on most women.

Men love a woman who is excited about their sport. If not, she should at least understand it or tolerate it. It sounds trivial but men are usually annoyed by a wife who really thinks the fanaticism of men is stupid, and would try to compete with sport.

I have even heard a woman accusing a man of loving soccer more than he loved her. Unfortunately, there are men who do, and of course they are idiots. But! Even *them* fanatics could reverse their loyalties if their wife was supportive of their love for the game.

One day just experiment with your man. Ask him to teach you soccer, rugby, golf and the rules, and watch a full game with him if you've never done that. Do it several times and see him suddenly warm up to you.

Women often express their sophistication by ridiculing men's obsession with sports, whereas to men, the sophisticated woman is the one who knows who Thierry Henry is and how prolific a goal scorer he is. I don't know why men are like that and I am one of them.

Remember, in the olden days, men used to be hunters and warriors. Today, we live in days of relative peace, notwithstanding the occasional wars the between the USA, the middle east and the north or south Korean islands. All of which I think is a bunch of man not getting enough All Bran Flakes - call it Cain and Abel Syndrome.

All this is evidence that men have had to divert testosterone energy elsewhere and I think it has all landed on Planet Sports. I will be the first to admit, it is very difficult to inculcate sports in someone who doesn't like or enjoy any form of healthy competitive sport; but I also do not buy the saying you can't teach an old dog new tricks.

I think that is an insult even to an old dog.

It's an issue of willingness.

I have dated a lot in my life, but I must say that the dates I enjoyed most, were with girls of diverse interests, especially those who could talk soccer, rugby, boxing, athletics, baseball, tennis and you name them.

I am a diverse guy myself and that helps. I am sports but then I am also a beauty pageants, *soapies*, romantic comedies and drama kind of guy. I also find interest in interior design and decor, fashion and music of all genres. In the man book I appeal to my stereotyped species that diversification of interests is imperative.

To women I am only talking balls for now.

'Wena le sokhanyana ye ya gago' is a stupid thing to say

The saying goes, if you can't beat them join them. You cannot beat men when it comes to their obsession with sports. Don't compete with that – frankly you're fighting a losing battle.

It takes a very naive woman to try to compete with men's love or even obsession with sports. You should see men during a world cup, any world cup. I bet if you check the calendar nine months after a world cup, you will find that the birth rate declines accordingly.

Women are the same. They have their own interests. I think I have made a great husband because somewhat I was in touch with my feminine side. I grew up very much involved with the things that my aunt was into.

She was into gardening and landscaping, interior design and decorating, cooking and all that. I learnt to do them all and became extremely good in some. I have found out in my relating to women, that those skills make me bond a whole lot easier with women than the newspaper reading man.

On the same breath, a woman who can cross over and breathe the air on the soccer field, especially the '*Xtra-Strong*' section of the stadium - SA colloquial for the stadium's public areas - becomes a greater woman.

I went to the stadium with a famous musician friend of mine. We didn't have suite tickets so we went '*Xtra-Strong*'. He brought with him an uppity girlfriend. She brought a fruit basket to the stadium. It was such a strange sight. I gazed at the basket and then looked at my friend and he smiled at me.

I know he had with him a woman who wanted to be better than 50 000 people filled in a stadium. At the stadium we eat pap and steak not a variety of exotic fruit.

In my mind I thought, this girl went through some bad upbringing, probably some absentee father.

But I must give her the props for effort.

She was trying.

'Together' is a powerful word

At one time in my relationship that became a marriage I was introduced to a very important word - TOGETHER.

Together is one of the most important words in marriage. It doesn't matter how compatible you two are, but sooner in the marriage you will find out that there are things you love passionately that he either doesn't love with the same passion or doesn't like at all.

The reverse would be true irrespective. So what do you do in such a situation? You chose to be with your heart – your love, your babe. You vote on the word together.

It is better to be bored being with the one you love than be entertained with someone you care little about. Actually if you do take keen interest you might just have fun.

If you cultivate curiosity and a multi-talented lifestyle you will discover that at a higher level of being and loving, there is no boredom.

I know men also need to come to the party on this one. It doesn't mean that you can't take that time to do something else that you enjoy. You should not feel obligated to endure the moment, just make time to get involved in the thing your man loves.

So your man loves soccer, rugby, cricket, balls in all their kinds, and maybe you do not tick like that, and you were not raised like that. What's your problem — you can't teach an old dog new tricks?

When did you become a dog and when did sports become tricks?

I love sports of all kind, I love soccer, golf, snooker, tennis, rugby and many other sports but I am still a very good man. I cannot become happy outside of those things. My interests are many and do take a good bit of my time. Some of those sports I have mentioned and some teams involved in the sports are not negotiable. This means that when those people are playing it's on my calendar.

I have taken leave from work for some of these events.

I know that I am an above average sports lover, but there are people I am no match to. When I watch local soccer on TV and I look at the Chiefs side on the grandstands, I see the same people whether the game is in Cape Town or Venda. They'd be putting on their academic regalia-looking outfits - B.Sc in Kaizer Chiefs I guess.

With Orlando Pirates you see the same people crying for the same reasons. Now those are the people I am no match to.

Imagine being married to one of those. If you live with the 'You and your stupid soccer' attitude, you are going to struggle unless you change your outlook.

Love Your Man with His Balls

When you marry a man, you marry him with his balls, and it would do you a world of good to learn them, ask about them, celebrate with him when he wins and pretend to mope with him when he loses if you can't do the genuine act.

Faking it is bound to happen especially in a marriage.

Besides, it has worked for you in other departments.

I remember a game when Orlando Pirates was playing Mamelodi Sundowns. It was an emotional game where I thought Orlando Pirates was being robbed. I was a Pirates supporter for that day. They are my second team, so when they play anybody but Chiefs, I stand on the tables and break glasses.

My wife came home and found me standing before the TV screen, screaming and threatening to kill the referee.

She asked, 'What's going on? I didn't know that Chiefs was playing today?' In essence, she knew, when Kaizer Chiefs was playing and she knew how I behaved when they were playing.

She loved the sports, she could go to the stadium with me, suites and '*Xtra-Strong*' alike, scream with me until she had no means to do so. But I knew very well she was not half as fanatic as I was.

She was simply being a great companion.

PASSION PROTECTORS

Life is exciting, even beautiful.

This statement and the truth in it is shared only by people who have passion for life or passions in life. Even people who have no passion for life do half good when they have passions in life. Your passions link you with the emotional part of your being.

The emotional man and woman in every one of us is absolutely necessary. Just like you can't go too far on this physical plane without your physical body, you cannot go too far without your emotional being.

Men and Women get their emotional release in different ways.

To women it could be shopping, watching soapies and reality TV shows, going to musicals or such like things.

As for men, they get their release generally through sports. It is important that those energies are released into your life and the poisons within are released out of it.

Recently I got so stressed, I lost the energy that people experience as Moss Mashamaite. My closest colleague began asking me if I was okay and I said I wasn't.

She asked 'Why?' And I said I didn't know.

'Do you have problems you may not be admitting to?'

I said I didn't - or at least none that I was aware off.

After a lot of soul searching I came out with an answer that I thought was not only as intelligent but divine as well.

I asked her, 'What would happen to a person who would work for days without ceasing or taking sleep breaks?'

She said that such a person would collapse.

I said, 'What do you call that?'

She thought for a while and answered rather aptly. 'That would be fatigue or physical stress.'

I said to her, 'Couldn't the same thing be experienced spiritually and emotionally as well?'

She said, 'I guess.'

And I said to her, 'Since I have no problem I can pinpoint, it simply means I need to recreate.'

I decided then to go on holiday. The one thing I did during that holiday is that I watched a lot of sports somehow, and I found this rather therapeutic. To be creative one has to allow for a life of rest, recreation and sports, especially for men.

Men and women that are in relationships are obviously in it to get some good into their lives, but it should also be for giving some good to the other's life. Christ himself said, 'give and it shall be given unto you in good measure, pressed down shaken together running over shall men give into your bosom.'

I once met a man who broke his arm trying to massage his back, yet he was married. As a result, the woman - his wife - couldn't go shopping because it cost a fortune to fix both his arm and his back.

A little giving would have gone a long way and saved a couple of bucks for shopping.

Allowing your man to get crazed up and support him in his *bally* world, is giving him the gift of relaxation, venting off and expressing his passion.

Ventilation and Respiration

Ultimately your man will thank you by just being a better and more relaxed person. More than all that, he would allow you to do the same in the way your gender and upbringing has prepared you for.

One of the reasons why people part ways and let things other than death do them part is their inability to create and nurture ventilating systems in their relationships.

Perhaps before people get married they should be counselled so that they understand life equals stress, experienced singularly by an individual but when individuals merge their lives together, the equation is not Stress + Stress equals two stresses but rather 1+1 = 11 stresses. Which is a totally different equation.

Therefore, the question should be asked to the couple individually, in the presence of their significant other — 'What is your principle diversion?' 'How do you detox?'

First member — shopping and musicals, plus a pyjama party with the girls.

Second member — soccer, boxing, rugby and an occasional Friday with the boys.

The wise counsellor would then advise, 'Now let us find a way to get these two respiration and ventilation systems together in a single unit of 'the two shall become one'. 'Let us marry the two principle diversions into one flesh.'

This alone could reduce the traffic towards the divorce court.

I have counselled a lot of divorcing couples and I have in many cases felt they were together as a couple, in a place where I had found myself in my stress narrative — accumulated stress and fatigue — reasons unknown.

Most divorcing couples when citing the reasons for parting ways, give symptoms instead of the actual condition. That is why therapists put them on the couch and ask them questions until the symptoms can be separated from the actual condition.

I have talked to couples who were divorcing and could tell you the reason just after a couple of minutes of starting a session.

Most are simply tired souls.

No recreation, no sports, no allowing each other to ventilate.

Trying to become one, they destroy all personal space until they suffocate the joy out of each other.

Going back to my theme in this chapter, and speaking with as much candour as you will allow me, I say   be the physician, even the therapist.

Do not only tolerate your man's sports, go farther and find a way to fuel it and encourage it. How about buying him a Sundowns fan kit for his birthday, or those Blue Bulls helmets with horns.

The results would be amazing.

It would probably be the best present - according to him, and it would be nice to see him coming back home from a win wearing the outfit.

MACAU, SOUTH CHINA

Not too long ago I took a trip to China, mainland, Hong Kong and Macau just to cure my being. Macau was an afterthought, maybe even a meaningful coincidence. I went to buy camera accessories in one Hong Kong store and luckily found a guy there, who spoke English perfectly well.

You struggle to find a fluent English speaker in China.

I guess the Chinese didn't get that colonized.

He asked me where I had been already, and I told him all the places and cities as well as tourist attractions.

He said, 'So you haven't been to Macau?'

I said, 'No, where is Macau?'

He said, 'It's a little island city state that has a whole lot of international gambling resorts. A vibrant night life and the works.'

He asked me if I liked to gamble.

I said, 'Not really, but if I am traveling and I sleep in a Casino hotel I occasionally cash some coins and wager them on a slot machine or so.'

'Do you ever Win?' He asked.

I said sometimes I do and sometimes I don't but it's been two years since I last gambled let alone win. I am not a gambler. I just play the machines the way children would play video games. I told him I'd like to go the Las Vegas of China for a change.

He told me how Macau was different and I just bought into the idea of escaping claustrophobic Hong Kong.

A South African passport can be a good thing to have. Luckily I did not need a visa for my coincidental trip to Macau. And so, the next day I got onto the ferry, speed jetted and sailed myself to Macau and was there within an hour.

I found myself in one of the most spectacular islands in South China. I was the only black man I saw - at least I thought I was.

Two things I found in Macau - plenty of casinos, with 'The Sands,' being the most monstrous and a huge shopping mall with all the top name brands displaying all wares you can ever imagine.

I went to the casino and played the slots. I lost 2,200 Hong Kong Dollars, which was equivalent to R2,200 back then. It hurt, but I concluded that since I was on holiday and one of the things you do on holiday is blow some cash - it was allowable to lose some money. What would a holiday be if you did not make misjudgments and lose some money? Imagine a holiday perfectly planned to the penny by your accountant? That would be so bloody boring it wouldn't be worth it.

So I took pride in the money lost and went for the next Macau adventure — shopping. Let's face it, the Macau gambling resorts like any others were built on losers not winners.

I then decided, the next time I look at the golden sparkle of The Sands, I will heave up air in my chest and proudly proclaim that I helped build it, or in the least keep it off the credit bureau.

So, off I went to the mall.

The wares on displayed were Gautier, Armani, Hugo Boss, Rolex, all expensive brands. My quick mind immediately decoded the Macau duality.

Gamblers go to Macau to gamble and those are mostly boys — risk-takers and sporty cow boys. Since this is an international destination, they mostly come with their women, and the only way they can pull of their sporty adrenaline-high-lifestyles is to balance things by making their women just as happy.

They give them credit cards and send them to the Macau Mall. To a woman, shopping - with a credit card *nogal* - happens in one fashion only — till you drop.

The man on the other hand, chasing his risky habits — the pot at the end of the rainbow, is also till eyes are red and he realizes that in sports there can only be one winner. In Macau, the winner is part of the landscape and the loser will soon be taking either a ferry or a helicopter to wherever the hell he came from.

In sports generally, even God doesn't know who the winner will be. He, having denied Himself voluntarily of the knowledge so He could enjoy the game like everyone else.

THE MACAU COMPROMISE

I advocate for every healthy marital enterprise to function in the spirit of compromise - the Macau compromise — I was reading through Siza's diary – my late wife – back then when I was penning this book and eyes fell upon her preparation notes for an interview at City Power.

She was later employed there as a Loss Control Administrator before she joined Chatworld as Vice President — her motto in life if she had been asked was — 'Live and let live,' and she did live by that premise until the final day of her tenure on planet earth.

She was facilitative instead of restrictive.

She died asserting herself, in that she asked permission from no one to live and express her beautiful self in the world.

I was with a friend the other day and we were dining. The food came with a lot of condiments and amongst them was chutney — and the brand was 'Mrs Balls' Chutney. He read the words as they appeared on the bottle and he chuckled.

I said what's the joke. He said, 'Mrs Balls' — that's the joke. I said, 'Wouldn't it be great if all the married women would be, in a figure of speech, Mrs. Balls.

He asked, 'What do you mean?' I answered, 'Wouldn't the earth become paradise if women would embrace their men's balls?'

He replied with an idiotic looking smile that confirmed consent.

"Every mother generally hopes that her daughter will snag a better husband than she managed to do... But she's certain that her boy will never get as great a wife as his father did"

– *Anonymous*

When you marry a man you marry him with his balls, and it would do you a world of good to learn them, ask about them, celebrate with him when he wins and pretend to mope with him when he loses if you can't do the genuine act.

Four

YOUR MAMMA

A well to do woman who had been through several years of depression decided she needed a vacation. When she discussed the matter with her husband he said he could go with her on a trip which he was planning to take around the world. She agreed and he added that he had planned to take his mother along.

She was not certain that she wanted her mother-in-law to go with them on a trip around the world. They argued about it for a while, the argument finally was a compromise — the three of them went on the trip.

One day when they were in Central Africa, camping out in the open, they arose in the morning, and lo and behold! The mother-in-law was missing.

They looked for her for several hours and finally found her standing in a cleared spot in a dense forest with a mountain lion ten feet away, roaring.

The husband cried, "Mary, Mary, what shall we do for mother?"

She looked the situation over carefully, meditated for a moment and said, "Johnny, it seems to me that the lion got himself into that fix. Let him get himself out the best way he can."

The moral of the story - most men will try to take their mothers with, on this two-seater boat cruise called marriage. Three things - most of the time, the mother will not refuse the invite. Secondly, they - mothers - are ferocious creatures. Thirdly, as ferocious as they are, they are probably the most protected species extant in the world.

'Your mamma!' - That right there is a swear word.

The biggest swear word in the world.

All swear words have one ambition when they grow up, to become as huge as 'Your Mamma.'

'Your mamma jokes' are notorious for being the most scarring and scathing humorous attacks ever concocted by mankind.

'Your mamma' is a nine lettered phrase in many languages and cultures, and in marriage, it is perhaps the worst phrase that a woman can say to a man.

In the African culture you can cuss at anybody anyway the gingivitis in your mouth allows. You can drag their private parts down the muddy alley all you like. You can even tell them about their father and all his scandals; the dirtiest stuff you can ever get on the cowboy. It doesn't even have to be true, but the ultimate, the no-go zone, is to cuss a person by their mother.

They can kill you. Literally.

Having lived in a multi-cultural society and being well-traveled, I would ask you to allow me to extend the mamma cord to the entire planet. It's not only in the African culture but in all the cultures of the world. When you marry a man, you also marry a whole lot of other people. Firstly, their mother, then their father, their sisters and brothers last.

These people usually don't like you and they may not for many, even contradictory reasons. They might just hate you because you are beautiful, but they could also hate you because they think you are ugly, or because they happen to know the person who would have made the right partner for their relative.

They could resent you for your intelligence, yet they could also despise you if they thought you are not.

I know a girl who has two sisters-in-law and she dislikes the one because she says the sister-in-law thinks she is pretty.

Usually when people say you think you are pretty it's them who think so. She resents the other because she says she is an MVV (Mooi Van Ver) — beautiful from a distance.

How do you help such an idiot?

Success in marriage includes succeeding with this social group, which are your new relatives. There are rare occasions where you find that they adore you and if you find yourself in such a situation, bless the Lord and reciprocate by looking after their son and solidifying the relationship.

This doesn't mean your relationship is not going to go through the dynamics that all social relationships go through. Therefore, if circumstances change, people might change. This means this advice is still for you even if you don't have these problems now.

Marriage and the Umbilical Cord

So once you are married to your man, be careful with his umbilical crowd. If he talks about them negatively, participate in the conversation with your ears. Bite your tongue! That little pink member is not safe. You should even go as far as defending them.

I must admit, there are man who have not cut their apron strings and these dudes are annoying. If you are married to one of those you are going to have to work twice as hard as the average woman.

Whatever the umbilical crowd your man has surrounding him, you pretty much knew about them before you married your man, so deal with it! Your job is to build bridges and not to widen hedges.

One reason longer periods of dating are preferable, is because you get to know your man better before you take a vow to live with him forever. You get to have the feel of the family that raised him too. Ideally, the family where a person comes from should also go into the decision of marrying the person.

I am not advising not to marry a man because you do not like his family. I am saying it's a package. You better make that decision knowing all the facts.

Love always overrules other things and you must just be ready to live with certain things if you overlooked them.

Of all these people, whom I call the umbilical crowd, the most important is his mother. This woman is untouchable, she can never be wrong, she can't even make mistakes. She is the voice in your man's head, the ideal woman.

Your man will always be the little boy and his mother, that guardian angel that fed him from her own body, in and outside of it. Trying to make that kind of creature to look bad or wrong, will take a whole bar of prosecuting attorneys working with you round the clock. Why do you think they call the planet we are living on, mother earth?

The one other reason you should never poke at his mother, not with a six-foot pole even, is because of your inherent closeness to your own mother. Sometimes a man can think that his wife loves her mother more than she loves him. Maybe most women do and the reasons are many. Her mother can never cheat on her with another person. She can never ask her for things she doesn't want to do, and even if she snores at night, she is usually too far away for her to be bothered.

The other day at the mall, I overheard two women talking about parents. The one said to the other, if they were to lose one parent, it had better be the father. 'Imagine living without a mother,' she punctuated. I thought that was an awful thing to say with a straight and pleasant face. There they were, killing their fathers just like that.

I thought it didn't really mean they didn't love their fathers, they just loved their moth more.

Compare Father's Day with Mother's Day all over the world. Statistically, the establishments that make those days as compulsory as New Year's Day, the commercial enterprises, make approximately three times more money on Mother's Day than they do on Father's Day.

Fathers are just as disenfranchised as fathers in laws, and in this chapter about in-laws we won't waste time on them. They are usually not a problem at all. Because you live in a glass house —the mamma house — your own mamma, don't throw stones at his mamma.

Your husband could tolerate the constant fear and doubt that you love your mother more than him, as long as you leave his mother alone.

Shaka Zulu had an almost romantic relationship with his mother, so did Alexander The Great. I mean it doesn't matter how great they were, the umbilical cord is the strongest physical connection your man will ever have with any woman, and unlike sex, she could never have that connection with any other woman.

Eve never had the same problems you have. Those are the perks of being a pioneer human being. In essence, what I am saying is, you must find common ground with your man's mother if you and him are going to be happy either as individuals or together.

I suggest you watch the movie, "Monster in Law" acting Jennifer Lopez. You could learn a couple of things I might be struggling to get across to you. One reason the young bride had to be easy on her mother-in-law is that she too is going to become one, some day.

Everybody and everything will make it a point that you and his mother are not on good terms. Most married women are comfortable in this position. It's a permanent cat fight. The old cat and the young cat forever at loggerheads. Nevertheless, this situation is not ideal for your marriage.

The old cat is suspicious of you. She usually doesn't trust you because she says she knows how bad women are. She suspects your motives because back in the day, hers were not noble. She doesn't trust you because she thinks you are typical. Everything she fears about you is true about her.

So the badder she is, the badder she thinks you are.

Perhaps H.L. Mencken was right when he said, "On one issue, at least, men and women agree, they both distrust women." Still you must make this woman your friend and you can. Speak nicely about her even if she's not too nice, because it makes marriage sense.

At least your husband will think more of you, which is good.

You must remember that the role of women or mothers is to nurture and to protect. They never retire from that office.

Two years back, Daily Sun reported that a man came back home one day and raped his mother. How does anybody ever do that?

A couple of minutes later his mother was stretching her old violated legs in her yard, trying to make sense of the events of the last couple of minutes. When she went outside she found her son, the same man that had just raped her, now giving it to the family dog. Real doggy style.

I don't know what went through her mind as she tried to figure out which was the worst event, but I will tell you this - If this same woman would be confronted with a situation, where a year later the same son came home with a woman to wed, she would inside her own still think the woman is not good enough for her son, the monster. That's how mothers-in-law are wired.

When the old fool thinks she has lost a son, give her a daughter and her son back, and she will give you your husband back. This is not easy but it's possible. The average person crumbles under diplomacy and generosity, and your mother-in-law is average, an average mother of an average grown ass boy.

My mother died when I was too young to remember her. So in my memory, which becomes my reality, she never bought me sweets, defended me, and did all the things that mothers are famous for, but I still love her like anybody does who has known his.

Hell, I lived inside of her for nine months and every part of my flesh and tissues grew out of her. When I entered her womb I was just a part let of sperm, totally invisible to the naked eye.

My father provided the DNA, which was just an architectural prototype and plan of what I could be, nothing solid at all — no material and minimum labour. Thirty minutes if I am lucky, hell I could even have been a quickie. One minute and a half! My mother provided all the material and all the labour - carried me for nine months - and suffered deformation of body in the process, even defamation of character since the circumstances of my conception were unaligned with societal norms.

I lived in her belly in total security, provision and peace. In brief, I am my mother and when you mess with dear mamma you are messing with me at a deeper level. Much, much deeper.

Married women must know that when you are messing with a man's mother you are messing with the essence of him. This includes even the stupidest of them.

As soon as I was born, I went straight to her nipple. That is why I think we all, men and women alike, later get obsessed with breasts.

My advice on in-laws is, you said you wanted to get married, it goes with the territory - part of the package. You want to be a medical doctor, you must be able to look at blood, and also be able to see people die. You've got to have the guts. It's an occupational hazard, deal with it! In-laws and marriage equals, occupational hazard.

You must have a strategy, a winning formula, to deal with this one. Diplomacy and wisdom must come to the party, otherwise you are screwed. During all the years of your life from the day of first awareness, through creche and early education, until the day you met your man you had plenty of interpersonal relationships. All these relationships were to prepare you for probably and usually the most difficult interpersonal relationship of your life - marriage, together with its appendage social relationships.

If at the point of getting married life has not prepared you, you will need to take a crash course — something like IN-LAWS 101 - would be a good start.

It is nice to talk to your colleagues at work during lunch and tell them how mean your in-laws are, and how they hate you — but whilst that provides lunchtime entertainment and feeds the rumour and gossip mill at your work place, it is not success on your part.

I would have liked to tell you that you should not get into that relationship with preconceived ideas, but I guess it's too late at this stage. We are now simply left with damage control.

Your husband must be enlisted on this one as an ally. He is supposed to be the first one to give you a breakdown of the personnel. So in a healthy relationship, he should become your partner.

In unhealthy ones they are usually not.

He may often feel he's been dragged between two hostile parties, where he is forced to make very difficult choices. I know you might think this extreme, but your mother in law is supposed to be your other mother instead of a monster. Nevertheless, to your mother in law you are mostly a suspect, unless she loved you before, as in a *pre-loved* contract.

When you have seen what is going around in marriages, you cannot quite blame the mothers-in-law. Besides, mothers-in-law are women, hopefully. I think it was Chris Rock who said that the reason why there are not many women Presidents of states when women are everywhere and forever the majority is because, women hate women.

Women have wily minds, you know that. Your mother-in-law has a wily mind and she knows that you do too. She has been out-thinking her husband for decades.

She has been the boss putting on the maid's uniform, and suspects that you are just as smart. So she must protect her son from what she's been doing to his father. So your diplomatic battles might just continue till kingdom come. On the father in law - The father in law is usually not a problem. In most cases when a man is old enough to become a father-in-law, he has been too long and too thoroughly out-manoeuvred that he is a toothless lion.

The older a family gets, the more matriarchal it becomes. Men get worn out by all the bickering and the nagging until they all just capitulate. When you go to your father for anything and all he says is, 'Ask your mamma,' it simply means that the King is off his throne - permanently. That's why this chapter will concern itself mostly about the female parent of your man.

Similar Situations, Different Approaches

A friend told me that when she met her mother-in-law for the first time, she said to her that she doesn't like her because she thinks she is smarter than her son, and therefore she will rob him.

When *lobola* time came, it was the mother-in-law who said that her son was too young. She was not protesting the age; she was protesting her person. It was just an excuse. But then again she is the aggressive type, totally confident and minces no bones about it.

Another friend with a different personality actually did very well, not only with her mother-in-law, but with the mothers of all the boyfriends she had ever been introduced to.

I asked her how she pulled it off.

She said, 'I start from day one. I do rope-a-dope.

I pretend a weakness, a softness and a submissiveness that is not native to me. Suddenly I look nonthreatening.

Next thing I meet the old woman's needs without trying too much. She said when she did break up with the boyfriends, it was their mothers who would beg her to stay.

Well you might say it's too late for you to get to that first meeting with your mother-in-law, but there is always a second chance.

People accept that people change.

Your mother-in-law should soon be saying, 'She has changed totally. I didn't even know that I could ever like her.' Such are the winning ways. Two women, similar situations, different approaches.

The winner in this regard said that she made herself her mother-in-law's daughter in a way that would make her own mother jealous - of course behind her back, and the battle is won.

These little juicy stories I got when I asked two smart ladies to join me on a weekend skiing trip in Limpopo. I told them I will pay for everything, and that I am writing a book about woman issues and I valued their opinions.

I was even told that mothers go as far as determining your man's erection. I asked why? She told me that one time when their marriage was going through a sexual drought, she complained to her mother-in-law. She said, 'Don't worry child, that problem will be sorted out.' The same night the man was a tiger in bed.

Tiger in bed? You ask! — Sorry I've never seen a tiger in bed, but can we just stick to that diction for lack of better words? She didn't know what the old cow said to her calf, but it worked.

I have been told tales and tales of varied situations, that I have come to conclude that the way into your mother-in-law's heart is through bribery.

I do not have another way to look at it or say it, but accept that as an honest advice from someone who has thoroughly researched this issue. There are of course situations where you find a mother-in-law who is different and they are not many. The general overview is that you should prepare for an old lioness that is breathing vengeance.

Have you ever watched Chinese martial arts movies?

They go like this, 'Master, they killed my mother and father and raped my sister, blah, blah, blah' or rather chang, ching, chong.

'Please teach me how to fight so that I can avenge their demise.'

The master agrees and trains the avenger. The End'?

Totally typical. Mother in law-daughter in law stories? Typical. Before your mother-in-law is a *mother in law*, she is a mother. As a mother she carried, nurtured and protected this baby for nine months in her body.

Ultimately the little one was born and became a baby, then a toddler, until he became a man. Suddenly the mother finds herself in a position where she has to hand over the project.

She has to hand over her baby to another woman, a younger woman, a less experienced woman, a newly mutated woman who could also have a different agenda, who could change the bottom line from nurture to exploitation.

The protecting and nurturing nerve still alive and well, the older mother's protective instinct could shift gears into the offensive mode.

So it is safe to conclude that the mother in law is prepared by nature to go on the offensive.

'*Your mamma offenses*' to your man are ineffectual to the sustenance of your marriage because they could confirm to your mother-in-law that you are the enemy.

So that you know, all your attitudes and whatever you say, are ultimately going to be picked up by your mother-in-law, through the *mother-in-law* radar. Yes, there is a radar that develops through the years and it can pick all things female, but even if it picks the wrong stuff the users believe in it totally.

'*Your mamma attacks*' are stupid and counter-productive. This is because the nine months' total connection between mother and child is bigger than any other connection you are ever going to have with your man.

The Evil of the In-Law System

The greatest anxiety of any young bride when they have to meet the in-laws is — will they like me? Isn't it sad? The whole in-law factory stinks and needs renovation. I wish I could write a book and make it compulsory for parents of eligible young men to read and memories before any negotiated nuptials.

You and I know that I am just saying that because I can't quite write such a book, you should rather let me talk to you. You have the right to be here and their son loves you — they can go to hell if they want to — you must retreat to your innermost person and tell yourself that you do not need anybody's permission and love, to be.

After saying that, be a diplomat, do what you've got to do to keep your own family functional by working on your diplomacy like your life depended on it.

WHAT TO DO WITH THE HOSTILE ONES

If your in-laws seem bent on undermining you and are blatant about not accepting or loving you, don't spend your life trying to romance a stone hoping it will melt. Rather try a life of minimum contact with them because that simply means, less confrontation, less hurting and less leakage of poisonous fumes into your marriage.

If people do not want to love you, don't hate them, but do not beg for their love either. Just be good and do what is right by them, and continue with your journey.

Your husband is supposed to leave mother and father and cling to you. The clinging clause is one of the things that should be thoroughly discussed in premarital counselling sessions. The would-be-couple need to clarify each other on how they understand this to mean.

It becomes easier to deal with inter-family issues when you are on the same page. The unfairness of the in-law factory is that mostly the woman's family accepts the man, especially if he is good to their child, whereas the man's family almost always look at their new bride as either not good enough or too clever.

Or just a gold digger.

Personally the whole gold digging thing confuses me.

In my book, women are allowed to be a little bit materialistic and I will tell you why. If a man and a woman go to bed and have sex, let's say for lack of better words he is a tiger in bed and somebody becomes pregnant with a child, it has been scientifically proven that ten out of ten times, it is the woman who is going to be with child.

If merely having sex for thirty minutes or even one minute and a half, means that you could find yourself with a life form to feed, to nurture, to raise and support - it would be stupid not to think economically about things.

The man who could later call you a gold digger, most of the times would be walking around town calling you names denying any knowledge of you.

As a father, the day my daughter comes to me and says she loves a man and she thinks of marrying him, the first question is not going to be, 'Does he make you laugh?' No, because laughter only puts bread on the tables of Eddie Murphy, Chris Rock, Kagisho Lediga, Trevor Noah and just a few other people.

My first question is not even going to be, 'Do you love him?' him?' or 'Does he love you?' because there is no currency or instrument of measuring that emotion.

As a father my first question is, 'What does he do?'

That is an economic question and it is a gold digging question.

To some extent, we are all gold diggers. Because we want to know that our child will be taken care off. As a married woman, it is your duty to test your man's ability to provide. If that means you appear as a gold digger to your in-laws, so be it.

It was the pre-eminent economist of all times, John Maynard Keynes who said, "We have been expressly evolved by nature - with all our impulses and deepest instincts - for the purpose of solving the economic problem. If the economic problem is solved, mankind will be deprived of its traditional purpose."

But don't we just want to be deprived of that purpose.

I must contest that the in-law problem is and remains primarily an economic problem, but *'Your Mamma'* remains a stupid thing to say.

Before your mother in law is a mother in law, she is a mother.

As a mother she carried, nurtured and protected this baby for nine months in her body.

Ultimately the little one was born and became a baby, then a toddler, until he became a man.

Suddenly the mother finds herself in a position where she has to hand over her project.

She has to hand over her baby to another woman, a younger woman, a less experienced woman, a newly mutated woman who could also have a different agenda, who could change the bottom line from nurture to exploitation.

"Children seldom misquote you. In fact, they usually repeat word for word what you shouldn't have said"
– *Anonymous*

Five

TRYING TO LOOK GOOD TO YOUR KIDS AT THE EXPENSE OF THEIR FATHER

I grew up in a balanced family of mother and father, and I also have a lot of friends with similar backgrounds. I went out to try to understand from people who grew up in mother and father families, regarding who between their father and mother they liked the most.

This question was asked of people in families, people who live in divorced marriages, and people who live in widowed households.

An overwhelming 77 percent chose their mothers, 12 percent

chose their fathers and 11 percent chose both parents. I did not stop there. My questionnaire went further to ask why.

'Why' seemed a very difficult question.

The final research proved that in most cases the children chose the mother based on PR — public relations - that's all.

The things that make daddy play second fiddle have not been proven at all. When asked, 'Do you think your daddy's coming home late is work related as against motivated by certain interests?' A great number conceded that they cannot really be sure of the veracity of that fact.

Have you ever asked yourself why most people love their mothers more than they love their dads? I will tell you the reason. I am sure if I asked this question in a big group, I would have as many answers as the candidates.

I think though, it is because most married women spend a lot of time (daily) telling their kids how good they are. That is not all, they also tell them every day how no-good their father is, until it sticks to their little brains and becomes fact, then truth, then their reality.

Mother plays victim and constantly communicates this to the children. The little time father spends at home, whatever he does, just seems to emphasize and prove how truthful mother's assertions are.

The last time I heard a daddy song was from Ricardo and Friends, and they were still little. It was such beautiful song. At the age of Ricardo, back then, in the eighties, most boys and girls still idolize their fathers and not without reason. The boys want to grow up and be like them, the girls want to be married to a guy just like them.

Then as they grow up things begin to change.

Not really things, things; but mommy begins to change.

Mommy soon realizes the children are old enough to engage in meaningful conversation with her. Sooner or later they become mommy's confidantes.

Mommy begins to tell them things she should be telling her friends at work or church, but old friends with similar situations.

Then the songs change and become all about "Dear Mamma" and

the daddy songs go from "Papa Was A Rolling Stone" to the late Kori Moraba's *"Bo Ntate Ba Bangwe Ba Ya Makatsa."*

Most married women need support groups for all the things they go through. Mothering, *wifing* and in-lawing, are too much for the average woman to handle. Even though most women are not average, they are only average and below when it comes to what should be spoken about and with whom.

The unfortunate part is that they use their kids as a support group.

'Your daddy comes home late, your daddy doesn't give me enough money; your broke ass daddy this, your cheating daddy that.'

'Your daddy treats me like sh#t.'

'Your daddy's sleeping with some whore somewhere.'

'I wonder where I would be if I had married Patrick Peterson, because he really loved me, and had wanted to marry me you know? That is if it was not for that Chantalle bitch.'

Suddenly your kids get to know that their daddy was not mommy dearest's first choice, and they wonder whether they were mistakes; and how they would really look like if they were now the Petersons - meanwhile the rant continues, 'Ask your daddy!'

This time ask him for what mommy knows the poor dude either does not have or what he won't give. They go and ask daddy and daddy doesn't or won't give. It goes to confirm all what mommy has ever said about daddy.

After years, and years of negative PR, the children end up thinking the old man ain't cool.

I have interviewed a lot of people and I am confident that my theory is true in more than nine out of ten cases. When the race of birth begins and a child is brought into the world, both parents have a hundred percent chance of being loved by the child. The child is full of nothing but love, and he will share it equally with his loving parents, and they do.

It is in the upbringing and what they keep hearing, where things begin to take a different form. It beats me why two people would get married loving each other, and then create beautiful babies, hell!

Even ugly ones, and then want to compete for importance in their lives, even for their love?

It's simply idiotic and women have to rectify this situation even more than men because they naturally get to spend more time with the kids.

The man will usually not correct the bad publicity because the poor dear does not even know it is happening. He comes home and everybody is quiet, nobody seems to want to talk to daddy anymore.

His name is now only mentioned as a threat.

'I Will tell your daddy!' Even though this gives him a place of authority it does not make him well liked by his own family — thanks to mommy.

Mommy the politician on the other hand looks good every step of the way. Mommy is winning the love battle and is looking better and better to the children. Sadly, at the expense of their father.

I listen to music a whole lot and most, if not all songs that are beautiful, from Tupac Shakur s "Dear Mamma" to Shirley Caesar's "I Remember My Mamma In A Happy Way," are about mamma.

Daddy songs? Rare!

Most married women use their children as a support group.

Before you use your children as a support group, as naturally as it comes, know that support groups are usually made up of a lot of messed up adults and your lovely children have no business being part of one.

Before you open your mouth about your man in front of your children, either to get their sympathy or to make yourself look good to them, just know that you are actually destroying your future generations' faith in the male species.

You are going to have messed up kids and you are planting bad seeds in your children's future marriages.

It was Ken Dodd who said rather sourly, "When I can no longer bear to think of the victims of broken homes, I begin to think of the victims of intact ones."

Let me break it down to you like this.

YOUR DAUGHTERS

I have dated people's daughters in my day and there is nothing like the serenity and confidence of a girl who thinks her father is the man. This is the girl with no daddy issues.

I am a father and I want to raise such a daughter and I am working hard on it. So far so good. But then there is the girl who has been told over and over again that his daddy is no good. She is usually too attached to her mother, to an extent that the man who marries her marries the old bag as well. Sorry for the old bag thing, it's not fair but it makes good writing and I am not trying to be fair but to write.

Such a girl also constantly needs mommy because men are no good anyway. The things you say over and over again to your kids stick — you should know the Pygmalion effect by now.

Indoctrination is so bad the victims seem insane.

Let me tell you a story. I met a white man who came to me and begged for money. I told him I didn't have any, but he had seen me buy something from a black guy who was selling Blue Bulls caps and I was given change after the transaction.

He said: 'But I saw you get change.' I was fascinated by the exchange because beggars are not supposed to be aggressive.

Begging is a form of selling where you sell something too soft for aggression — pity. Pity, like any other commodity is sold for cash. The pitiers buy it with money, and it's got no fixed price, it's like stock in the stock exchange.

The merchants of pity are not great marketers. They are geniuses. They dress the part, they do voice rehearsals and dress their words with pity. They act in such a way that Hollywood stars would be envious, and they make sure they stink as well, just to engage one more sense, the olfactory.

Now this man was breaking the unwritten rules of begging.

He was being aggressive.

I decided not to join him in the aggression.

So I said to him, 'You, sir do need spare change, meaning change I could spare isn't it?' He agreed and bought the loop and then I caught him.

'I did get change yes, but it's just not change I could spare,' I answered back. Like most beggars he was intelligent, so he got my point, but he was also a neurotic case and not suitable for the office of begging.

To beg you must leave your ego and its little baby eggs at home. The only spiritual part to begging is the subjugation of the ego. This guy had not gone through that course yet - or he could have just missed class that day when the rest of the begging world was doing BEGGING 101.

So he burst out. 'I am a white man and I am doing you a favour by begging from you. You should be grateful!' He exclaimed.

This is a true story - I might add.

Even today I am traumatized by the power of indoctrination. Can you blame the man really? No, blame his parents.

I did not want to deviate, I just want to stress how whatever you say to your children be they boys or girls, those voices — how they will never cease to whisper. It would take a miracle.

You could blame that man for being a lousy beggar but he was only performing the lines that he was given by the directors at the rehearsal — his parents.

YOUR SONS

Boys who grow up thinking that their father is the man exude a lot of confidence and they also know how to treat women.

They get manly advice from men and not from women, and they have the ability to ward off an interfering mother or family in their marriages or relationships.

Every woman wants to be married to a man who can tell his mother off and be able to take her side of things. The funny thing is that mothers, unless they are malicious and stupid, do not mind when their sons take a different view and protect their wives.

I know this from experience. I have had several strong talks with my aunt - spouse protecting talks. I've seen the smile on her face even when she would lose an argument, and she is the type that loved my wife to the extent that I could get jealous.

But she loved it when I was protective of her.

I think she thought in her heart, "That's how a man should be." Thinking of herself in my wife's shoes.

You must understand, I am not saying that men don't often deserve the bad rap. I am saying, 'Save the blab for people your own size, who have the software to handle the *bullsh*t.*'

Your children deserve to be raised well, with faith in the family, in you and in their father.

Do not be selfish.

Do not be narrow-minded.

Do not take your eyes off the big picture, even the future of your children. I am not saying that your husband is a saint and that everything you say about him is not true. I am simply saying you are talking to the wrong audience who would not help you solve your problems.

Instead, you are creating problems for them.

You are messing with their future. You must also remember that the damning PR is going to make your family less peaceful and your children less manageable and less respectful to their father.

Is that what you want?

You cannot try to build a happy home while on the other side you are destroying it one brick at a time. Make up your mind, are you engaged in construction or destruction?

In the year 2006 a South African soldier in the DR Congo, a member of the peace-keeping force, shot his big toe with an assault rifle.

As you might imagine, it was reported in almost every newspaper. Soldiers shoot the enemy, and how the toe attained to that status beats me. I don't know what the soldier was trying to achieve or what the toe had done to him, but one thing for sure; the enemy would be very pleased with his actions.

He was supposed to be on the side of the South African peace keepers, but there he was trying to finish off his own force one toe at a time, with that, charity beginning at home as charities should.

A repetition of that exercise would mean that all the enemy forces would have to do is provide the South African army with more ammunition.

The wife who has sessions with children, treating them like they were other married women and giving them the inside story of her relationship with their father, is simply being stupid.

I have a daughter with my ex-wife and in our entire relationship I have not said one thing negative to her about her mother. As much as this would please her mother, I am not doing it for her mother alone, I am doing it for me too, but most of all I am doing it for my daughter. I am also convinced that her mother is practicing the same wisdom when it comes to me, because all the good things that my daughter thinks I am, I discovered that she learnt from her mother.

When I came back home from the U.S. of A, my daughter fought her way to come and live with me. That could only be because what she had heard about me from her mother was just too great.

I must tell you that I think the most confused girl about why her mother and father are divorced and can't live together is my daughter. Personally I would rather she has that confusion than her thinking I am a monster, as according to her mother and that her mother is a monster, as according to me.

She is as healthy a child as we both want her to be.

So you can be a politician and score some points and look good to your children and make your spouse look really bad, but you must know, as green as the grass is green and as blue as the sky sometimes is, the losers in this scenario are going to be your own children.

If you really love your children and you understand that you have the divine assignment to carry them to a higher place towards their calling, you must change the way you do things, and how and what you talk to them about.

Keeping The Skirmishes at Home in The Bedroom

I was raised by my uncle and my aunt, his wife. I am sure they had fights of their own, but those fights were taken to the bedroom. In our presence they were lovers, and they did that for us.

Another thing that you must do for your children is to show them your love for each other instead of everything about you.

As much as you do not make love to each other in their presence for their sake, it is important not to make hate or war in their presence. Even the smallest babies cry when there is conflict between their parents. Instinctively they know it is wrong.

The healthiest men and women have probably heard their parents disagree, but never really seen them fight family wrecking battles.

Marriage ultimately gives birth to itself in the form its children and it must subsequently look after its creations instead of destroy them. I am not a naturalist, and I am therefore not encyclopaedic about species, but I am disgusted by pigs for the reason that they are one of the few creatures that can give birth to their babies and eat them thereafter.

A parent, be they man or woman who destroys their children in any and whatever form, is less than a pig because a pig is a pig.

It beats me why two people would get married loving each other, and then create beautiful babies, hell, even ugly ones, and then want to compete for importance in their lives, even for their love? It's simply idiotic and women have to rectify this situation even more than men because they naturally get to spend more time with the kids.

Marriage ultimately gives birth to itself in the form its children and it must subsequently look after its creations instead of destroy them.

"The woman is the home. That's where she used to be, and that is where she still is. You might ask me, what if a man tries to be part of the home — will the woman let him? I answer yes. Because then she becomes one of the children."

— *Marquerite Dams*

Six

WHERE ARE YOU AT?

We live in the age of the cell phone, a great invention that has increased our ability as humans to converse with one another. This was supposed to be a positive invention of all times, but like any good thing in the hands of man depends on how it's handled, the cell phone can be used as well as abused.

Electricity is both great and "dangerous, so is gasoline, alcohol, hell even the Holy Bible. People have hated, discriminated against others and even killed because of the misuse of the Bible and other Holy Books.

I would bet my life on the fact that in the last ten years, cell phones might have broken more marriages than booze. Yet at the same time the gadget has kept close relationships closer and even made loving and parenting a whole lot easier. It is not only the abuse of the cell phones that I would like to expose in this chapter though. In the City of Tshwane - previously known as Pretoria, I could cite you one hundred family break-ups that were caused by the way the cell phone was handled or mishandled.

I've got a magistrate friend who has been good to me with information about the latest causes of divorce. One might argue that it is not the cell phone per se that did death's dirty job. But that those marriages which were broken by the gadget were weak or were of cheats in the first place.

The argument might have merit, but it still does not deduct from the truth afore told.

The cell phone has declined from being the greatest innovation of the late twentieth century, to a stupid tracking device that spouses use to spy on each other, an instrument that has dealt the greatest blow to marital trust more than the Reality Show, "Cheaters".

For those people who have healthy relationships with their phones and their spouses, this might sound preposterous, but I must tell you, people out there are behaving really weird around the little gadget.

'Where are you at?'

This is the twentieth century question that could never be asked before the invention of the cell-phone.

The *pre-cell-phonic* woman never used to ask the frequently asked question. That is because she could only phone her husband when he was at work or at home on the land-line.

In itself, '*Where are you at?*' is made up of thirteen innocent alphabets, but it is a phrase usually used by the insecure married woman to put a tab on her man.

Don't get me wrong here, there is nothing wrong with that phrase and its use.

I am just zooming in on the insecure woman.

The cell phone has evolved from a communication tool to a tracking device. It's gotten worse with the new 3G and 4G technology.

Its maiden questions are, 'With whom are you?'

The woman here is asking questions of her man, to establish his geography, his sociology and simply if he is with any woman, or in a place where there might be women prettier than her.

The truth is, mostly when men are hanging out, there are women around. And no matter how pretty you are, if you must know, there are a couple of them prettier than you 'Where ever he is at.'

There are over three billion women earth and at least more than a million of them are prettier than you.

I visit the woman factory often, and I have discovered that every year, just like automobile and appliance factories, they come out with better models that are not only more beautiful but are even able to perform unusual feats better than the earlier models were capable of.

Is that supposed to make you insecure?

No.

When you met your man, there were still as many women on earth as there are today, almost. But he chose you. Trying to put a surveillance camera on your man is not going to help your relationship at all.

It is going to give you a lot of pain and it's going to give him a lot of pain too. Sooner or later because we all are trying to move from pain to pleasure, the obnoxious behaviour might actually chase your man away. And chasing him away is not only through divorce. It could also be through co-habiting or emotional divorce. Meaning, you drive your relationship to a place where you simply become room-mates.

Or you might just stress him to death.

Stress kills, and surveillance-camera-relationships are stressful. Perhaps your husband might be better advised to answer the obnoxious questions in this manner

'Where are you at?'

'I am on planet earth.'

'What are you doing?'

'Breathing in oxygen and out carbon dioxide'

'With whom are you?'

'People who don't ask stupid questions.'
'Why do I hear a woman's voice in the background?'
'That is because there is a woman's voice in the background.'
'Why are you talking to me like that?'
'Because you are talking to me like that.'
'I am your wife you know?'
'I am your husband and this conversation is over.'

Beautiful conversation rudely interrupted by the dropping of the phone. Very healthy for the man, and even the woman, as the beginning of therapy.

MTN, Vodacom and Cell C or whatever cellphone network you are using may not like the way the conversation is interrupted, but 'Where are you?' asked in those tones, must stop as of necessity.

It is doing you and your husband no good.

Just once, your husband should follow my advice so that you get to understand there is no need for keeping tabs. If you are convinced that your husband is up to no good, there are better ways to sway him and bring him home with a smile before it's too late, than to breathe on his neck with an onion flavoured mouth, or was that garlic?

Remember, a man is the hunter not the quarry, and therefore does not respond well to chasing aggression. Also note that the achieving energy of the female species has never been power or force.

Men are the aggressors who get their way through power or force, our biology has rendered us so. Women who try to do that, end up frustrated and losing out.

The achieving energy of women is influence or subtle persuasion.

Ask your grandmother especially if you are an African.

They never tried to overpower their men as desperately as they needed control. They simply bewitched them so they could become servile and subordinate. Even that did not always work. Some men became worse. Others stayed the same and the rest just went on a slow-down and became total morons.

In Loving Potions

Love potions are not an African invention. In Europe, Asia, the Americas, everywhere - women have been trying to make their men love and obey them more.

That chemical engineering has been employed throughout all ages. In my book, love potions are stupid because it makes no sense being loved by someone who is drugged by you.

Wouldn't it be better to know that you are loved naturally without any influence? Unfortunately, women do get that desperate until they lose touch with reality.

If you force your man to come home on a Friday night to spend forced time with you or which is rather more precise, to serve the marriage life sentence with you, what do you think you have achieved by that? Is he really with you, spending quality time or is he a bandit of the so-called love.

The only way to make people happy is to give them what they want. Sometimes you should try this on your husband.

'Baby it's Friday, are you going out?'

'Yea, like I said my colleagues were thinking of going to hang at such and such a place.'

'Okay, have fun. When do you think you will be back home, just so I know when to expect you?'

'Eh, I don't know maybe *elevenish*'

'Is it more like *twelfish*?'

'Well, you never know...'

'Don't worry, make it *one-ish*, don't be too loud when you get back, don't wake the kids up.' What might happen is that he could come home earlier than you thought.

If he comes later don't take him to task. He'll probably spend the next few days with you and if he does, make it pleasant for him. Make him think, 'east, west, south, north, is there really any place like home?'

You can actually persuade your man to love coming home and be home without bullying him into it or manipulating him through guilt.

You can get him home without annoying him and reminding him of things he knows, like: 'don't you know that you are a married man and a father of twelve children?'

Trying to Be a One-Stop Entertainment Shop for Your Man

Most married men are not free to go anywhere because their wives quarantine them. There's a new word in town and it's called 'VISA'.

Basically what that means is, if your woman is out of town or held up somewhere and you - as her man - are now free to roam around.

VISA is simply a man on roam.

I hear married men talk about visa and I pity them.

They have become prisoners of love and their prison warders, the wives, make sure all doors are locked. When I was not married, my greatest fear was to marry a prison warder. In my marriage with Siza, my late wife, I was never forced to stay home, nor did I ever need special permission to go anywhere, and that is why I loved home so much.

I have no issues with the place called home.

In fact I have developed an addiction for home.

The freedom of the city makes me love and like my liberator so much I have developed a habit of just wanting to be home.

Most women think if you want to have your man at home you must force him to be home and keep him under the shortest of leashes - the old ball-and-chain. I have seen a lot of men home and miserable and I have wondered how the woman could be happy when she knows that her man is so miserable.

It doesn't matter whether you are the best of companies and the greatest homemaker of them all, your man still wants to go out and be with his boys. He has a boys-need just like you have a girls-need. If you force him to stay home and not be with his boys, the day he breaks out, he may not be with the boys but with any girl who will represent freedom, just like the way you were at the beginning.

Woza Friday, Woz'umoya

Men love Fridays just like college students, and Friday may not be a day they want to spend with you. Friday might be for the boys. It is the happiest day of the week.

In fact, it's happier than Christmas or New Year, even their birthday. Men easily forget their own birthdays and they come once a year, but no man has ever forgotten a Friday, as many times as it happens in one year.

Your man might spend Friday with you, but he wants to decide how he spends it, where he spends it and with whom he spends it.

If you take over Friday from your man with your plans, if you tell him you need to go together to see some boring couple that is more your friends than his, you are mining your man's life.

Talking about couple friends - they don't really work.

Men prefer their own friends, not organized friends, and women sometimes think that their men need help in this regard. Organized crime might be more effective than any other type of crime but organized friendship is only effective for little children.

My daughter called me one day and complained that her best friend had dumped her and that she also influenced her other friends against her. So she didn't have any friends anymore.

I asked, 'none at all?' She said she had only one then.

Three days later when I asked how many friends she had, she said twenty-seven. How she organized that beats me, but her happiness on the phone proved the multiplicity of friends she had acquired.

She probably got a new friend who was a ring-leader of a group who subsequently linked her with her group. That does not work for grown-ups, especially *grown ass man*.

So it's Friday and you decide you want your man by your side, kicking and screaming, and suddenly your man finds himself with some boring guy discussing sports they both don't like.

One prisoner longing for freedom, talking to a fellow cell-mate about things that don't quite matter at that moment. Both guys know they don't want to be together. They are like kids who are forced to play together because their mothers went to school together twenty years ago.

A man without Friday freedom is simply unhappily married.

Take Saturday if you will, give Sunday to the family and their God, but give your man his Friday.

'*Woza Friday*' is a battle song for the battle weary male. If you are a smart woman, give your man his Fridays, and he will happily and voluntarily give you the rest of the week.

This sage of advice is not very easy if you are already into the habit of being a jailer. If you live in a world where you have already decided that your man cheats, and you have to guard him from himself and other women, you've got a bigger problem than you think. You might as a result try to jail your man and keep him as close to you at all times as possible.

Sorry, but that is not a marriage, it's a dungeon. I would like to tell you some things about jail - it makes people very innovative, it creates hardened criminals, and it changes good people into bad people.

Years ago I was employed as a Training Consultant for one of the big insurance companies in the country. I received a lot of marketers into the city for training. Most of them were married people. I observed the behaviour of married men amongst others. My observation made me conclude that the men who had freedom at home were more relaxed and better behaved. Those who were prisoners did the wildest things at night after classes. They visited all houses of ill repute and all exotic clubs in town and came to training the next morning with blood shot eyes and depleted pockets.

I lunched with them every day and I listened to their stories, and the things they did. It was shocking. They abused their freedom because they were not acquainted to it. So, 'mother-hen', be careful.

You might just be creating a monster that will later haunt you for the rest of your life, or somebody who would create escapades to live a secret life that you have made so enticing.

Mrs Houdini, be careful!

The main reason for insecurity amongst women is in that they often marry for all the wrong reasons. They easily marry a man they don't trust or even a man they don't respect, or a man they don't love at all.

When women reach a certain age unmarried, they begin to panic.

When their friends get married, their mothers begin to panic too. Now it's a panic party and most women will marry the nearest pants.

Poor pants!

'Poor pants' gets into the marriage because he was somewhat manipulated into it. If he's half-present in the marriage, the woman is stressed and her mother is also stressed. Now it's a stress party.

The two women, one experienced and the other her clone, now gang on Pants.

Poor Pants! I don't care how you got married, the fact is that you are now married and you must make it work.

Trust is a decision you make, and the day you discover that, you have evolved into higher forms. You are free and there is no imprisoning you.

Sidney Smith's got a point, "A good marriage is at least 80 percent good luck in finding the right person at the right time. The rest is trust."

Doses of Privacy and Intimacy Required

Giving privacy and intimacy in pleasurable doses is the art of loving, and those who can do that, will be able to turn marriage into a fairy tale affair.

The reason the cell phone has become a great point of emphasis in this chapter, is because it has become the greatest invader of personal space.

Cell phones have proven to be great tools for communication, but in the hands of the foolish woman or man they become weapons of mass imperative. Call these:

THE SEVEN COMMANDMENTS OF CELL PHONE USE

1. Your spouse's cell phone is his private tool of communication and it's got nothing to do with you. Respect it and stay away from it. Remember trust is a decision you make, not what another person does or seems to be doing
2. If your man s cell phone rings and he is not able to answer it, leave it — missed calls are allowed.
3. If your man leaves his cell phone where you can access it without him seeing you, exercise discipline and adhere to rule number one.
4. Eavesdropping on your man's conversations means that you and not him, need psychological help. The day this need becomes strong in your lungs, pull out your medical aid and go and consult. There is room for you in Floor Number Eleven of Louis Pasteur Building in Pretoria.
5. In your man's life there are and there will always be other women. They are colleagues, friends, relatives and acquaintances. In your life there are men from that same stock too. These people account for more than fifty percent of his cell phone population. The presence of these people in your man's life is an absolute necessity. Without them he would go insane. If you drive them out of his life, you must pull out a medical aid for him. Otherwise allow him to talk to them on his cell phone without your nose blocking all the air around him.
6. For the sake of relationship sanity, create cell phone off moments in your life, at will. The world can still run without you. Besides, people can leave messages and you can still get back to them.
7. Relax cell phone rules not only for other people's sake, but for your own sake also. Live and let live is a good rule for cell phone living.

"If Rosa Parks had taken a poll before she sat down in the bus in Montgomery, She'd still be standing"
  – *Mary Frances Berry*

Giving privacy and intimacy in pleasurable doses is the art of loving, and those who can do that, will be able to turn marriage into a fairy tale affair.

Seven

BEIJING

Allow me to begin this chapter by exonerating myself.

I will not, I repeat... I will not waste my ink debating the issue of the equality of women and men.

For a guy who was conceived in a woman's womb and ferried by the same woman for nine months, give or take; and thereafter raised on breast diet for months, to later in life participate in the frivolous debate of questioning the equality of men and women, I would be a damn fool.

Personally, I would consider it an honour, if that same woman who ferried and nurtured me, would consider me her equal.

Close debate!

It's funny but in South Africa, when you say the word Beijing people seem to know exactly what you are talking about, especially people born before 1978.

The name Beijing does not make them think of the capital city of the People's Republic of China. No, they think of an event that took place in that city in 1995 that revolutionized the whole world.

In a way of speaking, in 1995 women entered the world arena.

Feminism got a revival, but more than that, the institution of marriage in all cultures was shaken by an earthquake measuring 10 on the Richter scale. So before you flare tempers because Beijing is cited here as a stupid thing, give me a chance to tell my sorry tale.

I am a peddler of tales and in my culture a messenger is never killed until he has relayed his entire message. So chill for now, allow me to take you on a journey.

Beijing in my opinion had a great positive impact and an equally negative impact in the world. I must say though that the *pre-Beijing* world is giving way to a new form of enlightenment in the world.

I do not know if this has to do with the positive impact of Beijing, but the world has changed positively for womankind. I know it is not near enough and there are still problems here and there, but things are turning around.

Whether you are aware of it or not, the world is moving into the era of the recognition of the feminine element of being. Society is suddenly recognizing that it is cool and core to embrace the female element. We come from a west dominated era where the left brain was dominant, but reality and originality are calling.

When God created man He created one entity and called it Adam, which meant man or mankind. Within it in perfect balance, were the female and the male entities. It was the perfect specimen of being. God split the entity so that it could multiply itself and fill the earth.

Our greatest folly as a civilization is that we have lived our first seven thousand years repressing the female in us. The oldest cultures and religions survived because they nurtured the female element. Most of their deities were female. They worshipped and respected everything from plants to animals and things, because they observed the life force in everything.

Our present society is left brain and male dominated and if we are not careful, it's heading towards self-annihilation.

The naked pair of Eden, Adam and Eve gave birth to two children, one represented the male in us — Cain, and the other, Abel represented the feminine even though he was a man child. The masculine killed the feminine and almost left the world incapable of continuity and sustainability. This becomes an anecdote that summarizes the history of mankind till today.

I must start this chapter by admitting that in my opinion women are way smarter than men, and I am not trying to buy your face, you've already bought this book. We men, are inferior to women in many ways.

Man was made when nature was but an apprentice, but woman when she was a skillful mistress of her art.

Let me take you through a scenario where boy meets girl.

The woman looks at the man and her eyes go first to the marriage finger. Then she looks at his shirt and prices it. Prices the watch, the suit, the shoes and everything on his body. Let's say the price goes to R5 000.00.

Then she looks at his phone and the car keys and puts a price on them. All is done within the first sixty seconds at most. Then she introduces herself and asks where he lives. Whatever the answer is, she makes an evaluation and estimate of his home.

Then she might ask where he works and then there is an estimate of the annual salary and perks.

The man on the other hand during this whole period has looked at the woman's boobs and estimated the cup size. He has looked at the behind and the waist; and he is fully satisfied and licking his stupid lips.

This is one of the things that made me decide that women are a superior species to men.

Upon first contact men evaluate a woman on a Microsoft Powerpoint presentation, while women evaluate the man on Microsoft Excel spreadsheet, which does quick formulas and calculations and summarizes everything into a value.

I stood long amazed over this and tried to figure out by myself why this was so. Then I went to the Bible for some answers. I do not really know how we came to be, but I have decided to buy the story of Adam and Eve with several variations.

Since it doesn't make sense that God created the first two people and then they had two sons, and one son killed the other and then went away and got married somewhere, my version of Genesis would be that God created a couple of Adams and a couple of Eves. And that the biblical story represents the first experiment if we might dub it so.

I still do stick to the biblical version even with my variations.

I have debated the concept of our origin with scientists and theologians. In one meeting the scientists won the debate. So everybody came out believing that we were once apes that evolved into men.

I stood up and said; 'Well and good but who created the apes?'

Then someone said, 'They evolved from another life form.'

Then I asked, 'Who created that life form and started the evolution process then?'

It still leads to a Creator doesn't it?

I believe the superiority of women to men comes from our origin. Man was made out of dust; woman came out of an already living breathing entity, human flesh. I think that is how women got headway on men. Since dust was materially stronger and the first evolution was biological, and had to do with the survival of the fittest or strongest, men became the original rulers of females.

From the Stone Age to the present, man has ruled the fairer sex with great ruthlessness. Atrocities to women ranging from treating women as slaves or as children to abusing them physically and emotionally, have been the order of the day.

Depriving women of economic resources, education and everything else has spanned the seven millennia of recorded history. So women had the right to be fed up.

When Beijing came, female anger reached critical mass.

Beijing therefore became a morphological magnetic field of anger. Not only did the anger of women end up in Beijing, but it was spread broadly across all continents by the media and the wrathful disciples of Beijing. It is upon this background of millennia of untold atrocities, that the Beijing conference took stage, and appeared a loud mouthpiece for the suffering of women.

I sympathize with Beijing, but I do still have a bone to chew.

I probably must begin by explaining that the Beijing conference was necessary and on the dot of the matters as they were in the planet of dust. The issues that were touched were invaluable. There might have been a nerve of extremism here and there, but it never clouded the real issues. Women have been dealt the shorter end of the legendary stick for the longest time - if not since creation.

In my book, the first liberator of women was Christ, even though he was never really heeded. On Christ not being heeded, I am almost forced to agree with Nietzsche who said, "There was only one Christian and he died on the cross."

I am forced to agree with Nietzsche because even as you go through the Pauline letters, which became the very foundation of Christianity, you can't help but be appalled by the display of male chauvinism.

Christ would not have tolerated that.

Don't you think the reason the Christ (a male) was given birth to by Mary (a female) without the aid of a man was a message to mankind to strike the balance between the sexes? Think about it.

Earlier in his ministry Christ was confronted with a situation that Beijing would later have to deal with almost two thousand years later. Christ, in his ministry, addressed gender issues and treated women in an exemplary fashion for all to see, but he was not heeded because religion was and is still mostly chauvinistic.

Remember the story of the woman who was caught in the act of adultery. This is the first time in the history of adultery when only one person would be caught in the act.

Even masturbation would be shocked.

Or is he called *Master Bashin'*?

Christ did not ask who else was involved in this act of adultery.

I think he didn't ask because his society was so chauvinistic the human rights declaration was that the one under the missionary position - meaning, *Nando's Chicken* herself, would have to be sacrificed. The man had just been plucked out from the scene and warned never to touch this woman again.

Jesus was confronted with two issues, namely - religious hypocrisy and male chauvinism. There was also a human life in the balance, so he had to tread carefully. On the one hand it was a trap that could lead him to an early grave - or rather early cross.

He had to decide what would be the best solution for the moment, and which was the greatest ill that needed immediate correction.

Hypocrisy emerged as the first and most dangerous evil, and Christ had to deal with that first. It is hypocrisy that trespasses Christ's first commandment — *"Judge not, that ye be not judged. For with what judgment ye judge, ye shall be judged; and with what measure ye mete, it shall be measured to you again."*

Most if not all religious wars that have been fought or were fought because of the need for theological rightness than anything else. Sadly, most wars were religiously motivated.

The following is how the story reads as written in The Gospel according to St John Chapter 8: 3 - 9

> "And the scribes and Pharisees brought unto him a woman taken in adultery; and when they had set her in the midst, they said unto him, Master, this woman was taken in adultery in the very act. Now Moses in the law commanded us, that such should be stoned; but what sayest thou? This they said, tempting him, that they might have to accuse him. But Jesus stooped down,

and with his finger wrote on the ground, as though he heard them not. So when they continued asking him, he lifted himself up, and said unto them, He that is without sin among you, let him first cast a stone at her. And again he stooped down, and wrote on the ground. And they which heard it, being convicted by their own conscience, went out one by one, beginning at the eldest, even unto the last; and Jesus was left alone, and the woman standing in the midst.'

The second thing Christ had to deal with was male chauvinism.

If you follow this story, a woman was brought to Jesus who was said to have been found committing adultery. According to the law of the day, women who did that - commit adultery all by themselves, please - had a death sentence on their heads, and the men just walked away like nothing happened.

Obviously Jesus did not debate that, as in ask where the dude was. What was important to him was to save the woman from the situation.

When Jesus asks, 'Where are your accusers?' Meaning a bunch of Pharisees and scribes, it's clear that he was asking, 'Where are your male biased accusers who are accusing you of things they have done themselves and wanting to punish you with death just because you are a woman?'

These were a bunch of womanizers, rapists and human rights abusers who wielded stones, even rocks at women whose sins were committed with themselves.

The question again is, how was Jesus able to deal with these men until they left one by one?

I think it had something to do with what Jesus wrote on the ground. I believe he wrote what each of the accusers of this woman had done in the past several days with women, including the very same one.

On the ground, written by Jesus was simply, 'I know what you did last summer!' They left and the woman was safe, but how many had died before her. And how many more died after her.

All that said and done, you can appreciate the good thing that Beijing brought forth, but at the same time there was the negative side of Beijing that brought a lot of damage in the world and in families. The damage of Beijing was caused mostly by the misinterpretations of the people who did not attend the sessions.

Let me not assume that you know the whole Beijing thing and give you a background of what I am talking about. More than ten years ago, The United Nations convened the Fourth World Conference on Women.

It was September 4-15, 1995 in Beijing, mainland China. The purpose of the conference was to create a platform for action, whose aim was to achieve greater equality and opportunity for women in a world dominated by men who were blind to the existence of women except when it came to the gratification of their own needs.

Men raised by their mothers (women) who would grow up to abuse their wives (women). Some mass schizophrenia I might add. The official name of the Conference was "The Fourth World Conference on Women Action for Equality, Development and Peace".

The peace part is important to me because it means that women went to that conference knowing that there was a war taking place.

The war at home.

The war that had dominated the ages.

If weapons between the sexes could be laid to rest and rust, maybe the world would be a better place. Maybe!

This war according to women was for equality and the right to development. In my book, a holy war, a necessary war. The Conference was participated in by 189 Governments and more than 5000 representatives from 2,100 non-governmental organisations.

So the product that emerged out of that conference was broad-based and representative of facts regarding the state and status of women worldwide.

Nobody can mess with the truth that came out of Beijing solely on the issue of representation. The principal themes of the conference were the advancement and empowerment of women in relation to women's human rights, women and poverty, women and decision-making, the girl-child, violence against women and other areas of concern.

The consummating documents of the Conference are, "The Beijing Declaration and Platform for Action."

The overriding message of the Fourth World Conference on women was that the issues addressed in the Platform for Action were global and universal and long overdue. Deeply entrenched attitudes and practices that perpetuate inequality and discrimination against women, in public and private life, in all parts of the world had to be out-rooted and replaced by much more enlightened attitudes and practices.

Accordingly, implementation would require changes in values, attitudes, practices and priorities at all levels. So in theory and principle it was agreed that a new era for the recognition and respect for the feminine had entered the building.

Obviously I did not attend the conference in Beijing and I only know things from hearsay and research, but there is one thing I know for sure.

When women came back from Beijing they had attitude.

So I undertook to study some of the speeches that were given at that conference just to check them out. This is because of all conferences that changed the world, if you were to pick out ten in the entire history of mankind, Beijing would feature in that number.

It was universal, and it addressed and sympathized with the majority of all ages - women. The Beijing conference was all important in the entire history of our species, and whatever transpired there cannot and must not be ignored.

The Beijing Conference said to women that they are equal to men - which is true, even a truism. Unfortunately, it was interpreted by most women that it meant that they are the same as men.

'Equal' and 'Same' are not the same.

In importance the heart and the brain are equal, but they are not the same. The lungs and kidneys are equal but they are not the same.

Note that the mammalian body will cease to exist if any one of the organs I've mentioned failed. In the case of the heart and brain they are singular.

The latter work as pairs and one can't survive the demise of a pair.

That doesn't make the heart the same as the brain, nor the kidneys the same as the lungs. In importance they remain equal even while not the same.

The Beijing Conference went beyond equal; they went to further say that the Ying and the Yang were the Yang and the Yang or the Ying and the Ying.

Men folk and women folk complement and complete each other.

Beijing was interpreted to be saying; COMPETE WITH EACH OTHER.

The Beijing conference might have had a point or two, maybe a whole lot more points and merit, but it was dominated by women who were angry. Angry is not even enough. Afrikaans, help me out — they were *gatvol*.

If I try to pick fights with some of the Beijing speeches I am doomed to fail because they made some great points. Those points I will make and reiterate in my male version of this book, which by the way might also have Beijing as a chapter.

So to me Beijing was wrong, but it still had some valuable lessons.

In other words, the spirit of Beijing was wrong, but not its mentality. In fact, I think that they should have had a couple of men at the Beijing Conference who would be the male ambassadors to the female world. Perhaps some gay priests. People seriously in touch with their feminine side who could hear the struggles and problems and pains of the female species on this green earth of God Almighty.

I know somebody might be thinking, 'So you think it's okay for gays to become priests?'

My answer to that is, women went to Beijing; should gays go to Guan Zhou or Philadelphia?

In Beijing women got angrier than they were ever before. As they continued to share their situations of abuse and being undermined and ill-treated, their anger reached critical mass.

When the final word was spoken in that conference, and the women left the great hall for their respective countries, the anger spilled over from Beijing to the uttermost parts of the world.

This anger spilled even into innocent marriages.

Taking Marital Advice from Angry People

Bottom line, Beijing becomes a metaphor for taking marital advice from angry people, no matter how justifiably angry they are.

Most married women's marriages are fouled by friends.

According to social studies, the number one destroyer of marriages is bad advice. Maybe bad is too judgmental and I do not want to come across as that, let's rather use, unqualified advice.

Advice from people without a track record of success in the field.

When I was doing standard ten – Grade 12 for your millennium generation - and probably the most intelligent student at our high school and region, I was stopped from playing football by someone who was struggling to pass Standard Nine. I took life altering advice from somebody who couldn't advise himself to pass Standard Nine in thirty-six months and more, just because he had confidence in what he was saying, as stupid as it was.

As always, stupidity is sold in a package of confidence and passion.

That's how most people take advice from their friends whose relationships are worse than theirs. If you want to become rich you take advice from the evidently rich — you don't go to the guy who is begging at the corner of the street and say, 'Sir, I want to become rich, how do I go about that, can you help me?'

Funny how, when we want advice about how to keep our marriages strong, we go to people who believe that love is for the birds and marriage is a drag. In my search for answers, I interviewed a married woman whose best friends were two recently divorced women.

I asked her why them? Her response was that they were her friends, she loved them and she had the right to choose her own friends.

Needless to say, she is divorced now.

It was 1996 and the spill-over effect of Beijing Conference was on the rampage. The phrase, *'the right to,'* was in vogue. I knew then the quality of the advice she was getting - the namesake of a squatter camp — *Hlala Mpja*!

Her husband may have been a *mpja* in the Beijingers' eyes, but *hlala mpja* is too harsh even for a dog.

Why can't we benchmark from success?

I rarely see a married woman say, "Hey that couple has a tight relationship, I wonder what that woman is doing right. I want to make an appointment with her for counselling."

No, they go to the lady at work whose marriage is so messed up, even the security guards, all shifts, know about it; and then she goes about and tells them all about men. 'Men are this, men are that,' as if she was married to an entire football team.

You've got to be careful who you take advice from.

King David, the Psalmist in the very first Psalm says, "Blessed is the man (need I add woman) who walks not in the counsel of the ungodly..." In your walk, your talks, your fellowship, your company, including lunch and hanging out, you are being counselled even though the sessions are not formal.

You are getting advice from people who have passion and even pain about what they say and have experienced. So their stories are quite moving. But there is absolutely no need to make their experiences yours. You can choose who you hang out with them, or you can decide to qualify your counsellors before you engage them.

What success stories can the babblers you are listening to bring to the table? If there is none, then why are you listening and why are you taking notes? Besides, are you sure that they want to help you succeed in your marriage, especially since they are struggling themselves?

Love your Neighbour, and Know your Enemies

You may not like this, but sometimes you can be stupid enough to take advice from people who are jealous of you. In the words of Michael Korda, "No matter who you are, the basic truth is that your interests are nobody else's concern, your gain is inevitably someone else's loss, your failure, someone else's victory."

And Heinrich von Treitschke, the German philosopher of note, adds upon that when he says, "Your neighbour, even though he may look upon you as his natural ally against another power which is feared by you both, is always ready, at the first opportunity, as soon as it can be done with safety, to better himself at your expense."

You could easily be taking advice from people you think are your allies, yet only giving you advice to make themselves look or do better than you.

People go to school for several years to become counsellors, and even spend many years of trial and failure until they succeed, before they can give counsel with authority. The voice in your head, the tone of the loudest mouth about marriage and men — how many years did they study and what milestones have they attained in the field of marriage to qualify to give you advice?

Ever since I lived in the U.S. I've struggled with weight. I think it was the junk food. Besides, I had turned thirty-two and my metabolism had begun to slow down. Like most people, I was trying a lot of things to lose some pounds.

By most Americans' standards I was okay, but then I am a South African. The standards here are much higher. So one day I was at work talking about losing some weight when this seriously obese guy that I knew said to me, 'I know that I am not qualified to give you advice on weight loss, but I read a book…'

Right there, I interrupted him and said; 'Joe, I am a much more serious reader of books than you, and the last book I read said for me to tell you to shut up.'

White boy that he was, he turned red as everybody was laughing at the exchange. 'One hundred and sixty kilograms' was trying to advise seventy-five kilograms how to shed some weight.

Hilarious isn't it?

It sounds so ridiculous because you can see it with your eyes. Yet it is equally ridiculous when the unqualified marriage counsellor who has been in the field longer, is trying to teach you how to fail in marriage with unequalled confidence and you are listening.

A long while back I had an adoptive grandmother.

How she adopted me is a long story.

I went to Seshego, Limpopo to start a church. I was in my late teens. When I got the unction that I should go to Seshego to start a church and a "World Outreach Centre," I just took my clothes and my Bible, boarded a taxi and went there.

Somehow I never asked myself the basic questions of life – 'Where I was going to live and what I was going to eat.' I just followed the leading and went with the flow. As I was walking down a street in Seshego, lost in thought and doing very little logical thinking, I heard a voice calling from behind. I looked back and located the source of the voice to a little old granny in her late seventies known as Nelly — Grandma Nelly.

We knew each other of course, I had preached to her and prayed with her before.

So she asked me if I was Moshe (Moss).

I said I was.

She asked where I was going to and I told her I was in Seshego to start a church.

She asked, 'Where are you going to stay?'

The funny thing is that it was the first time I had thought about that — where 'the son of man was going to lay his head.'

I said, 'You know *ma'am*, I haven't thought about that.'

She said, 'Follow me to your room.' That room in her house became my home for many years to come, and when she passed on, she left that house on her will to me.

When I was twenty-two years old, a varsity student and pastor of LOD World Outreach Centre, I felt the need to go out there and make big bucks.

My older friend, Solly Matjekane was making a killing in the Life Assurance Industry, netting as much as R300 000.00 a month in today's values (2018) and I was inspired.

So I set out to become a sub-rep to him.

I went home to tell Grandma Nelly about my decision and she criticized me vehemently. She was very eloquent and according to the thinking of her day, there was something smelly about insurance salespeople. Crushed by an older intellect, I quit even before I started.

Many months later, I narrated to her a particular success story in the insurance industry. It was about a guy who dropped out from university. I had advised the guy to go into insurance. He took my advice and became very successful.

I forthwith reminded Grandma Nelly how she had discouraged me to do the same.

Guess what she said, 'You left insurance because of what I told you? How stupid can you be to listen to and be discouraged by an uneducated old woman? What do they teach you at the University of the North anyway?' And she left me there dumbfounded.

She was right. She was not qualified to give me business advice, but I had taken it nevertheless.

The Secret Behind the United States

Most countries were divided before they became countries or united. The United States of America, The Republic of South Africa, formerly the Union of South Africa and Estados Unidos de Mexico (United States of Mexico) were all divided before.

The funny thing about them is that it took wars to eventually get them to 'the united states.' And it will take a continuous and constant ideological war to keep them united. Likewise, the battle of the sexes dominates marriages.

Beijing was nothing but the metaphor. The Ying and the Yang exist at loggerheads. They are opposites yet they complement each other.

The battle frontiers within a marriage are manifold:

>> The battle of perceptions — seeing things totally different from each other — cold logic versus emotion and intuition

>> The battle of feelings — having conflicting sensual and other desires —I am horny; you are premenstrual

>> The battle of origins — my family versus your family. — You could be a Montague and I a Capulet, or you are Venda and I am Shangaan, or you are Xhosa and l am Xhosa.

>> The battle of opinions — what I think about certain things. Which could stem from my upbringing or maleness or femaleness

>> The battle of selves — What I need and what you need. You want to go shopping and compare items while Kaizer Chiefs is playing against Mamelodi Sundowns in forty-five minutes' time.

>> The battle of cultures — how we do things and how you and your folk do things. You are Zulu and I am Shangaan.

>> The battle of political affiliations. You are ACDP and I am SACP, or You are ANC and I am ANC

To keep the 'United States' united, the leadership reflects and briefs the President who would annually give the State of the Union or Nation address. Basically the union is kept together by two naturally conflicting mechanisms — war and peace broking. This must be done constantly.

So, Beijing was a war conference.

Women were on the war path and not without cause or reason. The problem with war is in that it is often harder on the innocent - the children and women in the literal sense.

Get me straight here — war in a marriage is not only necessary, it is inevitable. Therefore, it takes two diplomats to run a successful marriage. I advise that you enroll for diplomacy if you are going to be a wise married woman.

Your success in life is closely linked to your basic relationships.

That means, if you fail as a wife it will affect other areas too. If you are great as a wife, a lover and a mother, that is bound to add the flavour of success to everything else in your life.

Life is basically about the pursuit of happiness. Successful people are happy and happy people are successful, it's that simple.

Let's settle this, 50/50 vs 100/100

Today's woman enters into marriage already a victim of the Beijing mentality - that beginning of a 50/50 approach towards marriage. The 50/50 approach from an intellectual distance looks enlightened, but it is actually backwards. If I was a child and had a choice where to be born, I would choose to be born into a 100/100 family.

I would so refuse to be born into a 50/50 household that I would throw a tantrum before the Almighty that would make the big bang sound like the explosion of a Twenty Rand cracker.

I would rather be born in a 100/100 home in *Skuurlik* than be born in a 50/50 home in a golf estate. I am a thinking being and therefore my religious beliefs are constantly in drifting mode.

Sometimes I wake up doubting if there is a devil after all, but then I wake up the next day and I observe the turning of events in the history of our times, like the belittling of the institution of marriage by Beijing, and then my beliefs drift back — surely there must be a devil and he must be very sly and hard at work.

Sly because Beijing was legitimate and necessary. The oppression of women is an evil that society has perpetuated and tolerated far too long. But in the righting of that wrong by the angels of Beijing, demons at that same time crept through the back door and cut a good chunk of their own, out of the cake of matrimonial bliss.

Marriage was never to remain the same after the conference of 1995. I remember 1995 well because it was the year I got divorced.

Divorce was in the air and women who had dysfunctional marriages, some of which could have been healed, clustered and discussed the Beijing conference with little knowledge of the actual detail of 'The Beijing.'

It is not coincidental that my first marriage ended in 1995 after the conference. A couple of my close friends also ended their marriages in the divorce courts, and divorce lawyers could have made a killing if they were not charging R350.00.

The demise of my marriage was my personal metaphor for the spirits that were unleashed then. The lingo of the day has today become the name of a famous squatter camp - *Hlala Mpja* -Divorce The Dog. During that year, there was only one advice you got if you were a woman and you visited social workers' offices for counselling — *Hlala Mpja*.

I lived and pastored in Seshego, Limpopo then, and the Social Work office was in Zone 3 and it was nicknamed *Hlala Mpja*.

You came, told your long painful story with tears and mucus mixing into a mushy concoction. They listened to you and gave you a tissue paper without interrupting your long biased narration, and when you were through, they simply said to you - '*Hlala Mpja*!'

That was what social work entailed then.

I hope that profession has evolved into something better.

BREAKING DOWN 'HLALA MPJA'

Maybe let's break this *Hlala Mpja* thing into intellectual zingers that could be digested with ease.

The equality of men and women is a bonus to men because if you look at a woman as your wife, you can seek equality, but if you look at a woman as your mother you know that asking for equality is asking for a little too much of a woman who carried you with pain in her own body and birthed you in even greater pain.

There is no debating that, especially if you consider that in some cases her male counterpart was either denying any relation with you, or advising her to terminate you, or was simply unsupportive.

Nevertheless, the spirit of Beijing confused issues when it unleashed the inevitable anger of women on the institution of marriage. The only thing that salvaged the institution of marriage from the onslaught of Beijing, was the special love that women have for the married state.

From day one women work hard to get married.

They observe men and categorize them on the basis of whether they would befit the marital state or not.

Marriage will be perpetuated by that primitive desire to be born with one surname and die with another. Still, once in marriage, the modern woman soon resorts to the 50/50 approach, and she often takes advice from some old bag.

Need I say punching bag.

One that was married to some Mike Tyson and soon enough is the disciple of Judas Iscariot who would soon be willing to sell a good man for thirty Zim dollars.

Get me straight, it is stupid to be looking at your man and your marriage, and listen to the questions, and answer with this word – Beijing. After my tour of South China, I know that Beijing was the right venue for this great conference that changed the way the world looked at women, and the way women looked at themselves.

Our tour guide told us a lot of things we did not know about China, some of which were appalling. For example, because of the population having reached critical mass at 1.5 billion people, families were allowed to have one child only.

The fine for a second child ranged from one hundred thousand Hong Kong dollars (one to one with the Rand at that time) to almost half a million Hong Kong Dollars.

In agrarian states where the farms are the only means of sustenance, girl children became so unpopular that pregnant women would go to the doctor to check the gender of the child. If it was a girl, it would inevitably be aborted.

Even as our beautiful guide narrated this story, there was a sadness, almost a helplessness if not self-pity, on her face. The Chinese farming society was looking for strong creatures which would be able to farm and sustain them.

I could go on and on about how women were basically not appreciated in China and then you would agree with me that mainland China represented one of the worst case scenarios in the world's appreciation of the other sex, the fairer sex.

From another point of view, I am bewildered at men's mentality — thinking that marriage could work while working daily to entrench the inequality of the sexes, a doctrine that has been passed from generation to generation.

The roles we play in marriage are as important as they are equal.

The female is gifted and so is the male. So we should strive to combine the gifts to create balance in the family.

For many years there has been no balance. Beijing was meant to redress that wrong. With women having been hurt too much, the anger tipped the scales of balance until men were seen as — 'the enemy of the state.' In matters of males and females in relationships, I plead the biblical admonition that says, "Wives obey your husbands and men love your wives as Christ loved the church."

The obey - is about the man being the head of the family, but it only becomes possible and enjoyable if the man loves with unconditional, sacrificial love — as Christ loves the church.

Anything else constitutes abuse.

In other words, a woman should obey no less than a Christ-like lover.

RESTORING THE MAN AS THE HEAD OF THE FAMILY

When women came back from Beijing they were ready to wear the pants, and in most cases they did.

Somehow the conference had demonstrated to them that most men were not sufficient for the role of being head of the family.

I have lived around men and I have heard them say and seen them do such stupid things that I think that a lot of them are not fit to become heads of families. But let's do some reality check right here.

The position of husband is not like that of father.

Your father is like a King, he is born like that, to be that.

His place in your life is not debatable. You don't choose or vote for your father to be who he is in your life. So his authority over your life is unquestioned and undebatable.

Your husband is a different situation.

His authority or power is delegated authority, like the President of a democratic country. There are over two and half billion men on planet earth. You voted for one to become a husband and father of your children. That is your own personal choice, except of course in arranged marriages.

You looked at him and said, I think you have the wisdom, the resources, and the personal power to become the man in my life and possibly my children's lives. The unfortunate thing is that some women did marry their men knowing they were inadequate in all or some respects.

When those women heard the voices of Beijing, they soon demanded their own pairs of pants to put on. Men generally make a lot of mistakes, just like women, but they have been biologically evolved like in most species to be the ruling gender of the species.

It is sad sometimes that women put getting married as a first priority before assessing their candidate. There are situations where you see a couple and wonder how they came to be and how the man could actually be the head in such an unmatched relationship.

'How does a male hyena lord it over a Lioness?'

Such problems I cannot fix.

That is why in my attempt to develop our generation, I write young books like — "Ten Stupid Things Young People Say and Do" and "Ten Stupid Things Single People Say and Do."

Beijing wanted to dethrone the man because he was unqualified - he lacked either the wisdom or the sensitivity to run a home. To me this represents a societal dysfunction.

In spite of Beijing, the man must be restored to his position at the helm of the family by both his woman and himself, empowered by books such as my married men book and wisdom from such powerful contributors in the field as Ed Cole, author of "Maximized Manhood."

For those who feel unequally yoked with an inferior intellect, please find solace in the words of Vicky Aragon who said, "What it comes down to is that anybody can win with the best horse. What makes you good is if you can take the second or third-best horse and win."

The buck must stop somewhere.

The family cannot be a two-headed monster. Even if you were partners in a company and you were equally smart, it would pay to have a Managing Director. Even though you hold enough share value there must be one who holds the most responsibility.

Nature has dictated, that is the role of men. If yours seems totally incompetent, it would have to be blamed on you and nobody else.

You dated this guy, hopefully long enough to know whether he deserved your vote as head of your household or not.

That is all what the vows are about.

They are about voting for the President of your household. I do not advocate for female inferiority, I am advocating for peer-ship with appropriate roles. In my book, the word father is not superior to the word mother. Likewise, the words husband and wife — they are equal with different roles.

A women who pitches herself below the status of her man will fail just as dismally as the one who would like to take his role.

That is trying to fight fire with fire and people who do that end up with ashes. Nevertheless, if you really, and I mean really want to wear the pants, it's a free world, it's your pants and it's your pretty ass, and as I always say – whatever tickles your *Panty*.

"My husband and I have never considered divorce... Murder sometimes, but never divorce."
— *Joyce Brothers*

Today's woman enters into marriage already a victim of the Beijing mentality - that beginning of a 50/50 approach towards marriage.

The 50/50 approach from an intellectual distance looks enlightened, but it is actually backwards. If I was a child and had a choice where to be barn, I would choose to be barn into a 100/100 family.

I would so refuse to be born into a 50/50 household that I would throw a tantrum before the Almighty that would make the big bang sound like the explosion of a Twenty Rand cracker.

I would rather be born in a 100/100 home in Skuurlik than be born in a 50/50 home in a golf estate.

Eight

THREATENING YOUR MAN WITH DIVORCE

I have seen stupid things in my life and amongst them were women beginning to flirt with their ex's and turning them into their marital confidants.

A few things you should know about your ex, whoever he is:

1. He likes to think he is better than your husband and would actually like you to fail in your marriage so he could salvage his ego.
2. Your success is therefore bad for his health and your failure is good, even therapeutic.

3. Your Ex wants your marriage to fail such that if he had the magic to make it happen, he would apply his tricks to make sure it happens.

Why then would you go to such a person for counsel?
Are you stupid?
Okay there are exes that have no malice intended who might even wish you well, but flirting even with this kind is foolish, to say the least.

I think one of the causes of great disasters in human endeavours is how we choose our counsellors during difficult times. There is myopia around such times and one doesn't see straight, your lack of insight could be understandable.

Sometimes what really decides whether one is going to conquer or be defeated is who we choose to tell our sorry tales to.

If you hit rocky ground on your marital journey, of all people to listen to, leave out your ex. It might even be better for you to write a letter to dear Dolly - the anonymous woman who gives relationship advice to all kinds of people in Drum Magazine.

Allowing your ex to take you to dinner to blab away your marital challenges is a sad thing to do. Your ex might also think he has a hold on you because you went out with him and he paid a bill of R500.00.

I asked a woman who wanted to go on a date with her ex why she would to do such a stupid thing. Lo and behold, she gave me some stupid reason.

When I further inquired why they parted in the first place. She said, he had slept with her best friend after breaking her virginity. I told her, a guy who could sleep with her best friend would sleep with her mother if she would let him, and if she had a daughter, he would probably sleep with her too.

Hell, sometimes he might not even wait at all.

When I painted this image of a man with no respect for her to that extent - her friend, her mother and her child, she looked utterly devastated.

Then I said, 'He might even sleep with your dog.'

To this she couldn't bear, I saw tears filling her eyes - I thought the SPCA would really be touched.

I continued firing, 'Why would you want to eat out with guy like that? Are you that hungry? She laughed with tears still in her eyes. Long story short, she got my point and her ex never got to eat with her.

Stay Away from the D-word

If you want to divorce your man, do so, it's a free country; but if you still want to give marital bliss a shot, stay out of the ways of your exes.

I do not really believe in love back.

You can rebuild a car that has been wrecked in an accident but it could never be the same car no matter how good the workmanship.

It will always remain a rebuilt car.

In relationships, the things that broke you up become your constant insecurities. I know there are people out there who are making it out with their exes. I will tell you this – free of charge with a discount, they are exceptions to the rule.

Why am I mentioning this whole episode that seems so unrelated? It's because going out for dinner, even a cornflakes breakfast with your ex, without the knowledge of your partner; because sometimes it could happen if kids and legal complications are involved in which case you should inform your partner. If your don't, your actions can be the worst form of betrayal to your marriage.

It is a practical way of threatening your man with divorce.

If he finds out, he will be scarred.

Another stupid thing I have seen is a woman threatening her man with divorce before she even gives the D-word a thought. Remember, marriage is not a word, it's a sentence. A lot of women, when angry at their men, threaten them with divorce. If you want to leave your man you are at liberty to do so, but if you are not, please stay as far away from the D-word as possible.

That word is a curse to any marriage. And you must know one sad thing about men - their greatest fear in life is not you leaving them, at least not the man I know.

I was a widower and I cannot tell you how many times my married friends have said to me, if I was in your situation as in, single - I would do such and such a thing.

I got divorced at one time and one of my friends who was a parson called me a lucky man. So, marriage has turned men into wishful widowers and divorcees, and you think you are going to keep your man well behaved by threatening him a with divorce?

It might just backfire on you pretty soon.

Marriage Points

Most married women think divorce is some sort of joke, and the younger ones think they can just divorce their husbands and get another man to marry the with just a snap of a finger.

Do not be deceived by the multiplicity of guys who wink at you and profess love to you. They are not winking at your womanhood.

They are winking at your body. It's called lust.

They are lusting after you and undressing you so naked it's not even complimentary. You should be nauseated instead of smiling.

Do not act like you have downs syndrome.

Do you think it's cute to smile when you should be frowning? When one sees the 'ever-smiling people' that are ill it's pitiful and understandable. When you act similarly you confuse those of us who know what's going on. Sometimes women sit down and count all the men who told them they were hot in a period of one week, including the guy who helps them park their car.

After the count, the multiplicity of their suitors then raise their temperatures and they get home with an attitude. At the slightest provocation or argument, they say, 'I am going to leave you.' They forget that all those guys behaved the way they did because they wanted something.

The parking guy wanted some coins.

A good percentage of those guys were practicing their charm, and the rest of them were looking for a fling at the most.

None of them was looking for marriage.

And you want to leave a marriage because of them? Are you stupid? Because from where I'm standing, you must be confused.

Don't forget, when you get divorced you lose marriage points.

When you are young and pretty let's say you have a hundred marriage points – meaning, a guy might want to marry you.

His friends might advise him to marry you and his parents would be happy when he marries you.

Let's say every girl in their twenties has a hundred marriage points — which is our maximum marriage points. Men's marriage points are different and almost of no consequence. It's not fair but that is the reality.

Like I heard one wise Pedi woman say to a younger one, 'My child there are no ugly men. There are only two types of men. Men with jobs and men without jobs, their faces don't matter.'

Yet again, I digress.

Let's start at a hundred — and you are twenty-three, young, pretty, perky breasts, smooth skin, the works. To go above a hundred certain things might be required. Good education might put you at a place over a hundred but it might also - under certain circumstances - reduce you to below a hundred. Like when you are too educated and your man's friends and family think you might rob their friend or relative, blind.

Money can put you over a hundred and under rare circumstances can deduct from you. Personality is also another currency in this regard. It could place you at 100 plus or 100 minus.

So our sample *pre-marital* woman stands at 100, or 100 plus.

The average twenty something year old woman stands at an average of hundred. Let's say you look after your assets. Then you trade them in the market wisely and you get a suitor. He decides to marry you.

Now you are married, you do not need the points anymore.

You have actually traded them for lobola, dowry or a wedding ring. So let's be clear, a married woman does not have marriage points, in other words she is not desirable to be married.

I know people do marry married women, make them divorce and marry them, but to demonstrate that they do not have marriage points, society will attack you. Your family, your friends, your children or his children will get on your case.

Let's say you follow through with your threat for a divorce. Herein comes the calculation. When you divorce your man, you lose a total of about 25 marriage points and all your pluses with it if you had any. So before you say to your man, 'I am living you!' based on the winks on the streets, you must know that you are going back to the single world to campaign with a handicap minus 25 points.

Whoever you are going to meet might love you and decide that you are the right person, but let me tell you that before he makes his decision he is going to tell his friends.

And this is exactly what they are going to say:

'Has she been married before?'

'So she's got an ex.'

'So they had a little misunderstanding.'

'What if later in life the old flame sparks wildfire again?'

'Do you know, if they once were in love it means they still have feelings for each other? Come on man, can't you find some single person without baggage?'

Let's say he has the gift of the gab and you have a killer personality that makes his friends buy you with your seventy-five points. He still has to go home to his parents and family and tell them about you. And they are not easily pleased.

So they are going to ask their questions in this fashion.

'So she is a returned soldier.'

'She solved her problems with a divorce.'

'Hey and by the way, your uncle Joe says he knows Lucas her ex. Absolutely fantastic gentleman, he says that any woman who would divorce such a man would divorce any man, even Jesus Christ himself.'

'By the way, he says he *kinda* looks like Jesus himself, facially.' His exact words.

So here is your little man trying to sell heaters in a summer as hot as the summer of 2006, and you thought you were hot. Maybe you are, like a heater in the hottest of summers.

If in addition to having been married before, you have just one child, you lose another ten points. You are now at 65 and with any extra child you lose another ten points. In actual fact, you are going to be campaigning to a very hostile crowd, trying to get yourself married again.

I believe in miracles and I have seen a few people get married with zero points. But it's rare. Those are cases of absolute true love. The kind that makes true stories sound like fiction, but I would be unfair to give you advice based on the magical events of this life.

In most cases, women with zero points usually get married to a guy from Lagos - or whatever other nation - who just needs to be married to get citizenship.

As soon as you marry him and he is a citizen of this great nation of ours, he will treat you like sh#t or maybe just the way women are treated from where ever he comes, who knows?

I have never been to Lagos and I think that they did not send a delegation to Beijing. I may be wrong though, but I am too busy writing this book to take time to verify that fact.

Whether or not I have hit the nail on the head, you must understand that I still do have a nail and you do have a head. I have talked to a lot of men and women who went through divorce and I have discovered that the D-Word was flung around a lot, and mostly it was the women who did that.

'I am leaving you', 'I am going home to my mother', 'I am divorcing you,' etc. It might make you feel like '*the terminator*' and powerful but they are stupid words if you haven't sat down and thought about them and their ramifications deeply. That decision will affect you, your family, your husband's family, your children if you have any, and God knows who else.

So before you just speak like you are suffering from verbal diarrhea, understand the meaning of divorce and all that is entailed in it.

Talking about diarrhea, I think it is the most humbling thing that could ever happen to man. I can imagine being the President of the greatest country suffering from diarrhea during a fearsome crisis.

Tough!

Verbal diarrhea on the other hand is speaking because you have a tongue. Of all words that have to be thought over thoroughly before their utterance, I think divorce stands the loftiest.

'I do,' and 'I no longer do,' are perhaps the most serious phrases in the English language or any other language on planet earth for that matter.

I remember clearly that in my marriage with my late wife, Siza - we had our arguments and quarrels like any other couple, but never in our relationship, even during the most heated arguments did one of us threaten to bail out.

In fact, most, if not all of the times, we both apologized to each other for our role in the ugly moments of our argument. We did not have a lot of arguments, but when we did, we respected our marriage. We were at a point where we intrinsically knew that we were in it till death would do us part, and as painful as that has been, we have kept the promise to each other.

The day the D-word is blurted out it's like a virus has been unleashed on the relationship, a deadly virus.

Think before you speak.

No, let me rephrase — Think thoroughly before you speak.

In the olden days, divorce was very difficult because most cultures enforced marriage to be an eternal institution. The fact that men were the breadwinners and women were mostly home makers and economically inactive meant they were captives of their poverty.

Today's woman is economically active and some with even have more buying power than their husbands. This is freedom and it's supposed to be good.

As with all beautiful things, this freedom is often abused by women who think that they should hold loosely to their marriage ties by reason of being able to look after themselves.

The presence of money in your life is supposed to make things better and stronger instead of lending you the arrogance to speak as you will. Marriages must still be built diligently even though one has attained to a level of financial independence.

Good things like financial independence should be encouraged.

Yet people who attain to them must have the humility to be able to handle them. Great people are those who are able to dine with princes without losing the common touch.

You said you love your man and will hold on to him for better or for worse, in sickness and in health, for richer or for poorer.

Do that!

The financial empowerment of women is often made to look bad by women who think it means they are now husbands.

I had a business once in the U.S.A. with a partner. It was by far the largest appliance stores in Tulsa, Oklahoma. We made money and did well, but not too long the business went bad and we had to sell the store. An old man who was a friend of mine and extremely wealthy, also a client; came to my new store one day and asked me an important question. 'Why did your business as great as it was fail?' He probed.

I gave my opinion but he disagreed. He kept asking and I kept giving answers. All that time he would decline my answers.

A month later when he realised there was no wisdom coming forth from my thick skull, he told me it was because my partner and I never decided who was going to be the leader.

He said you've got great mechanical and technical skills; you should have become the Chief Technical Officer while your friend would become the Chief Executive. He would be the head and then the organization had a chance.

The fact that you were fifty/fifty partners did not mean you should both try to be top manager. The old man had a point.

When I grew up I was told that there was in existence a two-headed snake and l believed it.

Today if somebody were to tell me he saw a two-headed snake, I would ask him where, so I can see, because it would still be at the very same place they found it. Similarly, a two-headed family will not experience any progress at all.

When I was writing this book, back in 2007 – the ANC, South Africa's ruling party was engaged in serious political debate. The debate was whether the President of the Country should be a totally different person to the President of the ANC.

Some said it would create two centers of power.

Others said it is desirable because it will decentralize power.

I sat down and thought, and imagined a South Africa that had a powerful ANC with its own President and the country with an ANC President who was not the President of the party.

Then I called a Zimbabwean friend of mine and asked how many Zim dollars I would have to pay to get a Zimbabwean citizenship.

It ran into millions, but then again, who knows with Zimbabwean money these days? It could have simply been change.

My take, money or no money, the man remains the head of the family. And now that you are already married, I can't tell you the dangers of marrying an unresourceful man.

It is very important as a woman that you marry a man.

Essentially I mean that you should marry a man, and your man.

Women are good judges of both character and potential.

If you married your man because he made you laugh, but somehow you knew that translating laughter into food was going to have to be your next skill to master, do not suddenly seem surprised if your man brings home a plate full of jokes.

Look at what he brings in and multiply it by laughter and shut up!

THREATENING AN ABUSIVE MAN WITH DIVORCE

All I have been saying before applies to normal men in normal to difficult relationships, and yes, sometimes relationships are difficult.

Now I want to address a totally different scenario — an abusive relationship. Do not use the D-Word even to a man who is physically abusive to you. If a man strikes a woman, he is not striking a rock. He is striking flesh and blood, and you do not need such a man in your life.

Leave him.

There is no solution to a relationship where a man thinks he is Mike Tyson and you are some other equally tough boxer that needs an ass whipping.

I am giving you advice that I would give to my own daughter.

When she is married and she calls me one day and says her man beat her up, I will not enter into any negotiations with the boxer. I will enforce the termination of the relationship immediately.

I want to believe as a species, we have evolved biologically to a place where we can reason, debate, agree to disagree, have impasse's, even divorce, but I do not see a point in our relationship where on should use violence to drive a point home.

The civilized man does not communicate with force and should not be capable of such actions. If a man would raise a hand at a woman he is an animal, *pre-historic* Stone Age man.

He should go to the caves and live with apes. Give him a million plus years and maybe he might evolve into a human being if Darwin was anywhere near right.

Do not threaten the ape-man with divorce.

Divorce his stupid ass! If he comes back begging with tears in his eyes saying he will never do it again – don't. Too many woman have died on a second chance and therefore he deserves no second chance.

TO THE ABUSED WOMAN — 'HLALA MPJA'

You waz fashioned with hands of tenderness
You waz created carefully, specially and tenderly
Not from muddy clay but from the very bone of man waz you formed
You waz made to be handled with tender love and care
Not by hands of human beasts who suck a woman's breast
To nourish their early thirst and later thoroughly

Like thoroughbreds spew the violence upon women their nurturer
Though tough of spirit you are fragile of body
You are the proprietor of silky skin to be caressed
And not to be manhandled and ruffled
Oh woman you are the rose
The crowning moment and bloom of the garden of man
The mother of all the earth's children

You bleed every full moon routinely
Tell me, where are you going to get the extra blood?
If you willingly offer your body a sacrifice
You are condemned to monthly pain
Some say it's a curse from the garden of apples
Some say it is nature and was meant to be
Whether or not the loggerheads
Where are you expected to get an extra ounce of blood to shed?
Tell me, how much pain can you subject your body to?
Hlala mpjaf

With the bleeding that Women experience on a monthly basis it is wrong that any woman should be made to bleed by anybody.
That is why traditionally women did not go to war.

They couldn't afford more shedding of their own blood.

All that dandruff out of the way, always ask yourself the main questions, do you or do you not want to stay in this relationship?

Is it worth it?

If it is, retire your mouth from threats.

One reason you do not threaten this man, the ape-man with divorce is that he might just kill you before you do so.

MAKING YOUR MAN JEALOUS

There are women who go out of their way to make their men jealous. Obviously men also go out and do the same but this is not a man's book.

The purpose of making your partner jealous is one and singular — you are simply threatening him and making him understand that you are hot, and that there are men out there who are persuaded about that and are willing to do something about it.

Trying to make your partner jealous is a form of communication, but a weak form. The ugly part of it is in that it is rooted in low self-esteem from the person who practices it.

Any time you try to make your partner jealous you must remember and understand that all you are trying to do is to lift up your self-esteem.

Only people who are not independent of the good and bad opinions of others try to make their significant others jealous.

The problem is solely with you.

'The secret of being boring is to say everything'
— *Voltaire*

A lot of women, when angry at their men, threaten them with divorce.

If you want to leave your man you are at liberty to do so, but if you are not, please stay as far away from the D-word as possible.

That word is a curse to any marriage.

Nine

BLAR, BLAR, BLAR... WRITE YOUR OWN

"A man who marries a woman to educate her falls or victim to the same fallacy as the woman who marries a man to reform him."
   – *Alphonse Karr*

I am a rebel.
And chapter nine is my rebellion.

Ten

TRYING TO CHANGE YOUR MAN

Chapter Nine? You might want you know how you paid for 100% of a book that gives you 90% reading enjoyment.

I am a rebel. And chapter nine is my rebellion.

I am rebelling against all the chapter nines in all the books in all the libraries and bookstores of the world. Chapter Nine is yours — to write it and tabulate all the things you need to change in your life instead of other people's lives, especially your man's.

Finding Mr Right or is it Mr Right Now

You could say the single woman is perpetually looking for Mr. Right. Since he is a rare and elusive creature, they end up settling for Mr. Right Now with an initial — Mr. Almost Right. Sometimes they even outright, deliberately, eyes all open, in broad daylight, settle for Mr. Outright Wrong.

They drag this poor fellow to the altar with all the facts known to them. Then they spend the rest of their lives trying to right Mr. Wrong or change Mr Almost Right.

My take, whether you have married Mr. Right, Mr. A. Right or Mr Wrong, or Mr O. Wrong it is futile to try to change your man.

The only person that I know of, who came to earth to change people's lives is JC – some of you might know him as Jesus Christ. Even he had to spend three years with guys like Peter and Judas only to be shocked on the last day when the one pulled out a *panga* to cut a man's ear and another sell him for thirty Zim dollars.

If JC couldn't quite win the man-changing-game in some cases, to you I say, good luck.

I attended a funeral once, a sad occasion. The man had killed his wife while in an argument. It was a brutal affair. The man could not attend the funeral because he was in jail and he had been advised that his presence at the funeral would be in bad taste.

For some reasons only known in the circles of the law, this man was found not guilty of murder in the first degree.

Somehow they found a way to prove that a six foot three, one hundred and fifty kilogram man was defending himself against a forty-nine-kilogram woman.

Two weeks after this man was out of jail, he was already living with a woman who knew all about what had happened.

A woman who worked in the courts for that matter approached her to ask if she wasn't scared that the man would at some point do to her what he had done to his first wife. Her response was, 'He wouldn't kill me'. Meaning - he will change or I will change him.

She actually believed it was the woman's fault that she was killed, but deep inside, there should have been some fear and the panacea to that nagging emotion coming in just a few words - I am going to change him.

The First Approach to The Matter

There is one person, only one person that you need to change in this life, and luckily this is the only person you are capable of changing — her eyes are reading these lines right now. And if you look in the mirror, you might see her too.

To want to change your man you must first be self-righteous. Every time you try to change someone they immediately focus on you and the areas in your life that require change. Then you soon create a relationship with two people trying to find fault with each other. That could be messy and destructive.

I am a great advocate for change. I am also the first to admit that change is one of the most important mechanisms in the evolution of our lives. Yet change is personal and if you want to influence people towards positive change, you only do so by changing yourself.

The person in the mirror is only a reflection and if you look at the reflection and you don't like the shape of the hair — what do you do? Do you go to the mirror to effect changes or do you go to the person looking into the mirror?

Most times what you see in other people is simply the reflection of yourself. If you don't like what you see, look into yourself. I was asked to speak at my church, Higher Dimension Centre on the topic, 'Exceeding The Works of Christ.' My Pastor said that the church had quoted Jesus' words about 'greater works' over and over again and there seems to be only recital of the statement and no understanding. 'Can you join me in illuminating the congregation?' He asked. I agreed to do so.

The following is a summary from my presentation:

In his own words Christ is quoted to have said, "Those who believe in me shall do the works that I do, and greater works than these shall they do because I go to the father."

My task in preparing for this assignment was to find out what the works of Jesus were, that he needed us to exceed. I identified seven works of Christ as I was reading the New Testament.

Someday I will write a book about that topic, but for now I will just give you what I decided was the first work of Jesus - It was to get rid of condemnation religion. I derived that from the story of the woman who was caught in the act of adultery.

I've already told this story in the Beijing chapter. Here I want to focus on what Christ said to the woman's accusers — "He who is without sin, let him be the first one to cast a stone."

Suddenly there was no one without sin amongst them. To the woman he says, "Neither do I condemn you, but go and sin no more." My point here is, the only person who was not guilty of sin, the only pure heart was not condemning. The desire to change others has its roots in impurity on the side of the change agent. The purer you get the less you are inclined to judge or want to change other people.

Another reason why a woman might feel inclined to change their man has its roots in the reason why they married the man or rather how she got him hooked onto her. If you married him for all the wrong reasons, when those reasons become no longer important, then you are going to be in trouble. I was watching the soapie 'Generations' and the character Sibusiso Dhlomo married the character Karabo Moroka because she was pregnant with his baby. The baby died almost as soon as it was born. Then what?

The Female Stages of Entry into Marriage

There are four stages of entering into marriage for women – and these are:

The stage of innocence — teen age. Then there is the age of love — early twenties. Then the age of pressure — late twenties; and then the age of dismal pressure — thirties and above.

At each of these stages women many for different reasons, and it is these reasons for getting married that determine women's behaviour while married. Let me break these stages down categorically for you.

ONE: THE STAGE OF INNOCENCE

When women marry during their teens they usually don't know what the hell they are doing, or what they are getting themselves into. When you are in primary school you think the guy you love in your small pre-menstrual female mind is going to be your husband.

Even boys think so too.

And like in the fairy tales, you are going to live happily ever after with him. At teen age that idyllic dream has not disappeared entirely. The only difference with the premenstrual female is that now you can even be persuaded to marriage by physical pleasures.

I know there are cultures where most women enter into marriage at this stage, and though they do manage to raise families and their societies have not as yet collapsed, the women of such societies are simply victims of a chauvinistic lifestyle of antiquity.

For such cultures I prescribe Beijing.

Beijing was responsible for many divorces where women had been enslaved by fear and did not realize that you choose your own life. Arranged marriages fall under such systems.

Of course some women get married at this stage out of sheer stupidity or circumstances such as pregnancy or even poverty. These are creatures who will never know the beautiful sides of love. The innocent do not try to change their husbands nor their circumstances. They are simply captives, slaves.

The only reason to marry someone must be love and like. Personally I rate like just as highly as most people do love.

TWO: THE STAGE OF LOVE

Most people who marry in their early twenties marry for love, which is the one reason they can stand alone to account for the 'Whys' and 'Wherefores' of matrimony. These are beautiful relationships and if they do work, they work really good. The problem with this stage of entry is that it happens while love is still blind.

Blindness being sometimes curable, problems can emerge with the first opening of the eyes.

Sooner the woman might realize that her husband is a totally different species. Or an idiot, or a philanderer or that love, no matter how powerful and heartfelt, does not pay the bills. At this stage, most women have not self-actualized. So they might have fallen in love for all the wrong reasons.

The immature stage of seeking love is trying to find your opposite other — meaning introverts going for extroverts, etc. Because you have not accepted yourself and you are still dealing with issues of self-image, you find yourself attracted to people who don't look or behave like you.

In my experience opposites do attract, but after that they attack.

Following the biblical rendition of the origins of man, the Holy Book says that after God had created Adam, he left him a while until he felt very lonely. It was then that he decided to create for him a woman.

Adam was made of clay, the very soil we daily tread upon. But when God was to make Eve, did He go to the ground again? No, He went straight to Adam and cut a portion of his body. His rib to be to be precise, and formed a woman out of that. Same species, same person, same type. And what did Adam say when he saw the woman for the first time. With a boner between his legs, Adam sang the original anthem of erotic love - "Finally bone of my bones, flesh of my flesh." It's good and noble to many out of love but it could also be tragic.

Like, is a bigger factor in sustaining a marriage than even love.

Love is the trigger of course but like, is what will keep the ball rolling. I once watched a movie where a young lady who was about to marry a young man was trying to sell her guy to her father. The old man said, 'This guy of yours scarcely went to school and it seems like he doesn't even have a straight job.

Tell me, why do you want to marry him so much, what is it that you see in him?'

The daughter said, 'Daddy I love him, and he makes me *lef* (laugh). That's when the father angrily said, 'Chris Rock makes me *lef*, Eddie Murphy makes me *lef*, Murphy Brown makes me *lef* but you don't see me marrying them.' When blind love's eyes begin to open and you now see clearly at 20/20, then you try to change your man. All the things you didn't see before are out in the open, glaring.

Trying to do something about them by changing your man will bring about so much conflict in your relationship it could destroy even you.

THREE: THE STAGE OF PRESSURE

During their late twenties women get under pressure to get married. Their families put them under pressure (sad) and the big Three Oh (30) exerts even more pressure. The fear of declining fertility, if they believe they should have kids only after marriage, puts them under even more pressure to tie the knot.

So they are more likely to marry any guy who can sing the 'Will You Marry Me' ditty. In the process of hustling for the diamond ring, they are likely to chase away good potential suitors because marriage pressure is a repellent to guys who feel like they are in charge of their lives, and want to do things in their own good time.

So being desperate, they get to marry another desperate person.

A desperate guy.

Do you know how pathetically desperate a desperate guy should be? Mr. Desperate is 'torn up from the floor up.' The girl, at an earlier age is looking a standard of ten out of ten, but may end up marrying a guy who scores a measly four or at best a six.

And what does she say to herself? — "I will change him."

During the age of desperation, the woman wants to marry not only for all the wrong reasons, but also for all the wrong people - your family, your parents, your society, your church, and if she has any children she is looking for a father for her children.

In other words, men are now interviewed on the basis of what other people think or want. Suddenly there is an interviewing panel.

Parents can pressure their daughters into marriage so much they will drag any two legged creatures into the house and even pay *lobola* for it.

They would buy two rings and two wrist watches, and have the wedding of the year with it, even though they know pretty well that there would be no marriage following the wedding.

At this stage there are reasons to get married and they go like this.

1. **He's got a steady job.** And it might be necessary at this stage to categorize steady job. It means any job where the employees are required to put on a jacket and a tie, an overall qualifies only if the job is with the government. If he also drives anything that uses gasoline or diesoline, even natural gas, that is a steady job. And this is irrespective of the education level and intelligence level of the woman as compared to the man. In my book there is danger when a woman sits in her closet and thinks of her man as inferior whether financially, intellectually or in any other way, because such man is not going to get to the place of head of the family in the psyche of the woman. And a man is only the head of the family in so far as the woman thinks so in her mind.

2. **He seems to like children.** This conclusion is not made over a scientifically viable period of observation. Just hugging a dirty kid with the subject wearing a white shirt and get soiled in the process, but still look like it was nothing, qualifies the man for the — 'Seems Good with Children' title.

3. **At least he goes to church.** I have actually heard a born again Christian saying this about a guy who had promised marriage to her — "He loves the Lord; he is a man of God." And when I asked what church he went to, she spoke with the straightest face I hadn't seen since the death of Die Ou Krokodil (P.W. Botha) - "ZCC." Let me explain to you that cats and mice will hang together, braai some meat and even drink single malt whiskey before the ZCC and *Abazalwana* can be friends. By the way this has nothing to do with the ZCC, it is the *bazalwanas*. They judge the ZCC, not vice-versa. This *mzalwana* girl called a ZCC man, a man of God.

4. **My children like him.** As if he was going to get married to them.

5. **He is corresponding with UNISA.** I like UNISA but I think corresponding with UNISA has been an abused status in South

Africa for many years. Stupid people who were corresponding with UNISA were given the status of intelligence. I personally know a couple of certified idiots with UNISA degrees even. Back in the day stupid teachers were promoted to principals or deputies because they were corresponding with UNISA. I can remember a couple of certified idiots who got married, on 'the corresponding with UNISA' ticket.

FOUR: THE STAGE OF DISMAL PRESSURE

A woman at this stage lowers her standards to a point where she doesn't even ask questions of the guys interested in her, fearing that she might not like the answers.

They lower their standards to - if he is not gay, if he brushes his teeth at least a couple of times a week, if he is employable and has a driver's license, then I will marry him.

I will make him over and clean him up.

So she goes ahead and hooks up with him and cleans him up with Sunlight Liquid, Handy Andy and then polishes his weather beaten skin with Mr. Min himself.

Or is he now Dr. Min with a PhD from UNISA?

Problem is, Mr. Cleaned Up doesn't know what the woman thinks about him. He thinks he's a hit and because of that, he might even develop an attitude when you try to change him.

The problem with changing a person is that it makes you superior to them. It's like a man who takes a woman back to school.

Why do you think such marriages are destined to break up?

I personally hardly know of a situation where a man took a woman back to school and they are still together. When she comes back to you with her degree, she looks at you and thinks in her heart, he thinks he made me. Therefore, I must be forever grateful.

The next thing is, she looks for somebody who didn't know her before she got the *education*. Somebody who would meet her and say wow, you are smart, instead of someone who would be thinking dammit, that's my English she is speaking through her nose.

The same happens if a woman gets a man who has nothing, and

tries to set him up in business. When he succeeds he is not even going to cheat on you. He is going to divorce your ass. He will look at you and when you expect him to be grateful; he will despise you for what he thinks you are thinking about him. He will go out and find a woman who knows him as a bad ass businessman, a self-made man.

He wants to boast and it is not quite going to sound right in your presence. This just shows you how bad it is to try to change people because, even if it is for their betterment, they will soon resent you. Besides, you have got inherent in you, the temptation to one day open your mouth, and tell them how they were nothing before they met you.

That threat alone could traumatize him, and he could leave you.

Bottom line; do not try to change your man.

The Bottom Line

The bottom line is never to get into a marriage with a change agenda, but if you are already in a marriage, you must abandon all effort to change your man and begin on your very own self-improvement exercise.

You will realize that as you change yourself into a better person and into a higher being, suddenly all things and people around you take the form of you.

The Second Approach

The second approach should be to acknowledge the differences and live around them. There are, I believe several things that even if you were Jesus Christ, you wouldn't be able to change in someone else.

Things like - their personality.

It is just so sad that people get married to people whom they hate so much. How a person could marry somebody whose personality they do not like baffles me.

Sadly, enough people do so, and you might be one of those.

So you knew what you were getting yourself into or maybe you didn't, but *okusalayo* you are stuck in this and have to find your way around it.

The way around changing things is changing yourself.

Soon you will become happier with yourself and people will feel better around you.

Before you think about it people will adapt to you without any effort on your part. I will close this final thought with the words of Farrah Fawcett who said, "God gave women intuition and femininity. Used properly, the combination easily jumbles the brain of any man I've ever met."

You could say that the single woman is perpetually looking for Mr. Right. Since he is a rare and elusive creature they end up settling for Mr. Right with an initial — Mr. Almost Right.

Sometimes they even outright, deliberately, eyes all open, in broad daylight, settle for Mr. Outright Wrong.

They drag this poor fellow to the altar with all the facts known to them. And then they spend the rest of their lives trying to right Mr. Wrong or change Mr Almost Right.

This is not a book for married woman only. It is a book for all women, because women whether married, single or divorced remain primarily woman.

About

The Author: Moss Mashamaite

MOSS MASHAMAITE is a businessman, a writer and motivational speaker. Some people have dubbed him the social critique or political commentator. What you'll find though is that he is more of a poet, a novelist and often a humorist and satirist.

He is renowned for his hilarious, poignant and provocative style in speech as well as the written word. He's got a truly mighty presentation, one that you will find is irresistible to ignore.

His books in particular are simply not the kind you want to put down because he writes the kind of books even people who do not like books find it hard not to read. A literary artist, an educator and a powerful motivator that's who he is - Moss Mashamaite

Moss is a graduate of the University of Limpopo where the influence of his ideas was greatly felt by all the came into contact with him. He holds a qualification as an Educator and Degree in Biblical Studies and History. After successfully completing his degrees he went on to further study Engineering with Harcourt College and later earned his PhD in International Trade at Columbus University.

At the time of writing this thought provoking book, he had enthralled more than 100 000 audiences filling speaking engagements for organizations such as, The African National Congress, Uganda Authors' Forum; Metropolitan Life; Pick and Pay; Victory Fellowship, Road Accident Fund; Proudly South African; Felicia Mabuza Suttle Show; Department of Minerals and Energy; Department of Education; Eskom; Nu-Payment Solutions, West Rand Mall Business Owner's Association; Higher Dimensions, and many others.

His other stupid books include but not limited to:

>> Ten Stupid Things Grown-Ups Say And Do, It's Official There Is No Cure For Stupidity

>> Ten Stupid Things Young People Say And Do, It's Official There Is No Cure For Stupidity

>> Ten Stupid Things Married Men Say And Do, It's Official There Is No Cure For Stupidity

>> Ten Stupid Things Married Women Say And Do, It's Official There Is No Cure For Stupidity

Most women lose their men mostly for stupid reasons.

Most women realise a couple of years later when they get to meet other men that they actually had a good deal, a better deal.

Other Stupid Books

...BECAUSE, IT'S OFFICIAL THERE IS NO CURE FOR STUPIDITY

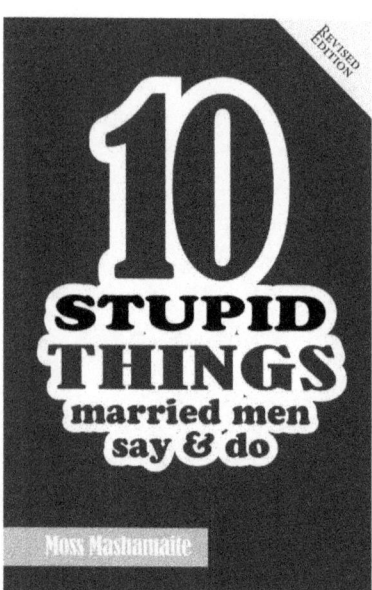
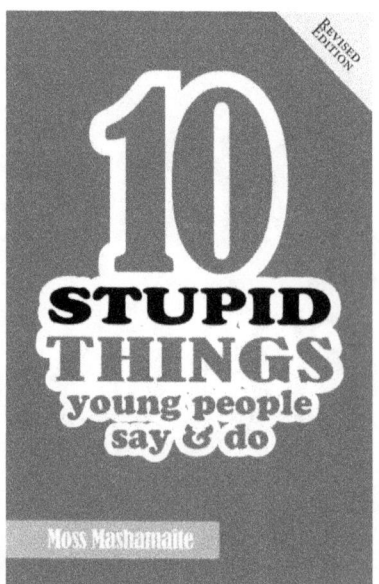
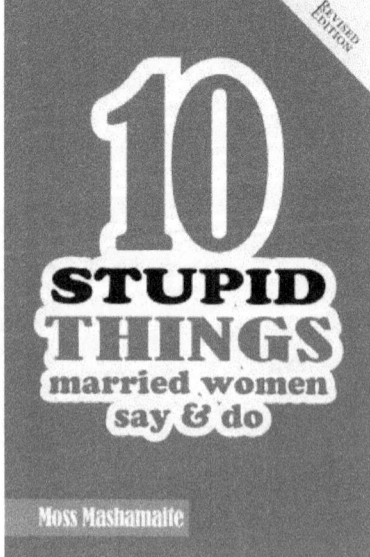

www.ingramcontent.com/pod-product-compliance
Lightning Source LLC
Chambersburg PA
CBHW022105090426
42743CB00008B/722